# LARISSA BEHRENDT

Larissa Behrendt is a Eualeyai and Kamillaroi woman. She is an academic and award-winning author, and is currently a Professor of Law and Director of Research at the Jumbunna Indigenous House of Learning at the University of Technology in Sydney. Her first novel *Home* won the 2002 David Uniapon Award and a 2005 Commonwealth Writer's Prize. Her second novel *Legacy* was released in 2009 and won a Victorian Premier's Literary Award. She is also the author of several books on Indigenous legal issues. In 2009, Larissa was named NAIDOC Indigenous Person of the Year and in 2011 she was named NSW Australian of the Year.

*To Jilpia Nappaljari Jones—who found her way back to her country with such grace and dignity*

AUSTRALIAN SCREEN CLASSICS

# rabbit-proof fence

## LARISSA BEHRENDT

CURRENCY PRESS,
SYDNEY

NATIONAL
FILM
&SOUND
ARCHIVE

First published by Currency Press Pty Ltd and the NFSA in 2012.

*Currency Press Pty Ltd*
Gadigal Land, Suite 310, 46-56 Kippax Street
Surry Hills NSW 2010 Australia
enquiries@currency.com.au
www.currency.com.au

*National Film & Sound Archive*
GPO Box 2002, Canberra
ACT 2601 Australia
www.nfsa.gov.au

Reprinted 2019, 2020, 2024.

*Australian Screen Classics series:* ISSN 1447-557X

*National Library of Australia—Cataloguing-in-Publication Data:*

| | |
|---|---|
| Author: | Behrendt, Larissa, 1969–. |
| Title: | Rabbit-proof fence / Larissa Behrendt. |
| ISBN: | 9780868199108 (pbk.) |
| Series: | Australian screen classics |
| Notes: | Includes bibliographical references. |
| Subjects: | Rabbit-proof fence (Motion picture). |
| | Motion pictures, Australian. |
| | Feature films—Australia—History and criticism. |

Dewey Number: 791.4372

Cover design by Katy Wall for Currency Press.
Front cover shows (from left) Tianna Sansbury as Daisy, Laura Monaghan as Gracie and Everlyn Sampi as Molly. Back cover shows Everlyn Sampi as Molly and Tianna Sansbury as Daisy.
Typeset by Katy Wall for Currency Press in Iowan Old Style roman 9.5 pt.
Printed by Fineline Print+Copy Services, Revesby, NSW.
All images within the text are reproduced with the kind permission of Phillip Noyce and Christine Olsen

Currency Press acknowledges the Traditional Owners of the Country on which we live and work. We pay our respects to all Aboriginal and Torres Strait Islander Elders, past and present.

# AUSTRALIAN SCREEN CLASSICS

## JANE MILLS
Series Editor

Our national cinema plays a vital role in our cultural heritage and in showing us at least something of what it is to be Australian. But the picture can get blurred by unruly forces such as competing artistic aims, inconstant personal tastes, political vagaries, constantly changing priorities in screen education and training, technological innovation and the market.

When these forces remain unconnected, the result can be an artistically impoverished cinema and audiences who are disinclined to seek out and derive pleasure from a diverse range of films, including Australian ones.

This series is a part of screen culture which is the glue needed to stick these forces together. It's the plankton in the moving image food chain that feeds the imagination of our filmmakers and their audiences. It's what makes sense of the opinions, memories, responses, knowledge and exchange of ideas about film.

Above all, screen culture is informed by a love of cinema. And it has to be carefully nurtured if we are to understand and appreciate the aesthetic, moral, intellectual and sentient value of our national cinema.

Australian Screen Classics will match some of our best-loved films with some of our most distinguished writers and thinkers, drawn from the worlds of culture, criticism and politics. All we ask of our writers is that they feel passionate about the films they choose. Through these thoughtful, elegantly-written books, we hope that screen culture will work its sticky magic and introduce more audiences to Australian cinema.

*Jane Mills is Associate Professor & Deputy Director of the Journalism & Media Research Centre at the University of New South Wales.*

# CONTENTS

## ACKNOWLEDGMENTS

With thanks to: the inspiring Jane Mills for her patience and friendship; researchers Amanda Porter and Terry Priest; screenwriting gurus Simon van der Borg and Ross Grayson Bell; Simone Herbert-Lowe and her eclectic cinematic knowledge; my mother, Raema Behrendt; and my husband, Michael Lavarch, who also knew that the stories of the stolen generations had to be told.

# I
# A STORY WITH RESONANCE

Simple stories are often the most powerful, and the story of *Rabbit-Proof Fence* is one of the simplest.

In 1931, fourteen-year-old Molly Craig, her sister Daisy, aged eight, and cousin Gracie, aged eleven, were taken from their families at Jigalong in the Pilbara region of Western Australia to the Moore River Native Settlement, a mission on the western Australian coast some 135 kilometres north of Perth, where they were to be trained as domestic servants. Longing for their families, they escaped and, while being chased by the authorities, walked across more than 2000 kilometres of desert back to their home, following the rabbit-proof fence, a massive pest-exclusion fence that crossed Western Australia from north to south.

There is much about this story that resonates for me but the strongest is the need and desire to find one's home, one's sense of place and one's sense of self. This is a universal quest but for Aboriginal people taken from their families, as these children were, that search for home, that need to feel complete, is all the more powerful.

## Family resonances

My father had a document holder, a red one with clear plastic sleeves, and in it he placed all of the papers that were important to him. In it he had his parents' marriage certificate and his mother's death certificate. There were entries from trust accounts of his mother, Lavinia, whose wages had been recorded while she was working under the supervision of the Aborigines Protection Board.[1] There was a photograph of her in her family's camp, taken before she was removed. In it, Lavinia is a dark girl, perhaps about ten years old, with eyes like my father's. She wears a white long skirt and a too-big blouse. She is sitting on the ground cross-legged, a slight slump in her back.

But in pride of place in the front sleeve of this plastic red folder was a copy of my grandmother's removal certificate, the piece of paper that recorded her being taken away by the Aborigines Protection Board in 1917 at the age of eleven. This piece of archived paper was important to him because it was one of the few things he had that connected him to his mother. It was also important because on that paper were the clues that had assisted him in finding the family from which he had long been dislocated. On it was the place of his mother's birth, Dungalear Station, a pastoral property just out of Walgett on the road to the opal mining town of Lightning Ridge. There was also the fact that she had a brother and it recorded his name—Sonny Boney. Armed with just this information, in the early 1980s my father headed out to northwest New South Wales to find his family.

This folder of documents was really a book of my father's treasures; he carried them with him and they were among his most important possessions. As he grew older, anything that connected him with his family, especially his mother, seemed to take on additional importance and significance.

When he finally found his family, he arrived three months after his uncle, the Sonny Boney listed on his mother's removal certificate, had passed away. So

Everlyn Sampi as Molly, Tianna Sansbury as Daisy and Laura Monaghan as Gracie.

there was no reunion. Instead, his uncle's angry widow greeted him. She demanded to know why he hadn't turned up earlier. It turned out that Sonny had been looking for Lavinia, his sister and my grandmother, his whole life. That he died just three months before my father knocked on his door struck me as a reality more bitter in its irony than any piece of fiction could be. It was a vignette so deep with human tragedy and loss that it was one of the core parts of the story in my first novel, *Home*.

In this novel I also wrote about an incident that was central to my own life. It was the time that my father took me to Dungalear, and I stood on the very spot from which my grandmother had been removed. It was a profoundly powerful moment, one when I felt that the story over my family over several generations had come full-circle. I felt at that moment very strongly how deeply resilient my Aboriginal heritage was, how it had survived through the attempts to assimilate my family.

I was drawn to *Rabbit-Proof Fence* not simply because it was an Aboriginal story. It is undeniably one that has a special significance for Aboriginal people, both because of their connection to their traditional country and because so many had been removed or dislocated from it. My grandmother was removed. There is no doubt about it. There is a 'Removal Certificate' to record the event. My father knew he was Aboriginal but, having grown up in an orphanage, he didn't know anything more about his heritage than that. His need to find his place, his land, his people, drove him. This story of removal was a central narrative through my family history. It is a central narrative in the family histories of almost every Aboriginal person I know. But growing up, in the southern suburbs of Sydney, little was taught of this history.

In fact, nothing was. The children I went to school with were good kids but many found my need to identify with my Aboriginal heritage confusing. And some held views that were shaped by deep ignorance as much as prejudice. I felt, even then, that if the schools taught more about the history, impact and legacy of the government removal policy, even if it didn't completely soften views about Aboriginal people, it would at least deepen understanding of the issues facing Aboriginal people, their families and their communities today.

## Bringing them home

In 1995, Labor's Attorney-General Michael Lavarch commissioned an investigation into the policy of removing Aboriginal and Torres Strait Islander children from their families. The investigation and research was extensive. By the time the *Bringing them home* report was handed over in 1997, it was to a different government, the Liberal-National Coalition Government led by Prime Minister John Howard.[2]

Laura Monaghan as Gracie and Tianna Sansbury as Daisy.

One of the most powerful aspects of the *Bringing them home* report is that it contains a large number of excerpts from the evidence given by the people who, as a direct result of the policy, had been removed as children and by the parents who had lost their children as a result of the policy. The stories of what so many people endured is more moving and persuasive than the statistics, the explanations of the policy and the exploration of the ideologies that underpinned them.

And while that report went some way to raising awareness of the issue within Australia, the film *Rabbit-Proof Fence*, with its simple story of three girls walking across a desert to find their way home, took the story of the stolen generations to the world.

# 11

## DORIS PILKINGTON'S LONG JOURNEY

This is a book about a movie adapted from a book. Doris Pilkington Garimara is the daughter of Molly Craig, the eldest of the three girls whose journey she writes about in *Follow the Rabbit-Proof Fence*. To understand the movie, it is essential to understand Doris Pilkington, her life and her writing. For me, the movie was always an extension of Doris and her story. I was drawn to her and her writing. It was her book that resonated with me before I came to the movie.

Doris tells her own story in another book, *Under the Wintamarra Tree*. There she recounts the story of her premature birth, under the tree of the book's title. She was so small when she was born that she could fit in a shoebox and it was believed that she would not survive. But not only did she prove everyone wrong by clinging to life, this little fledgling of a baby girl would survive and grow to be a strong woman with a remarkable life and a powerful voice. As her birth perhaps foretold, Doris's life was not going to be easy. She was born on Balfour Downs Station, a pastoral lease and cattle station located about 132 kilometres northeast of Newman in Western Australia's Pilbara region, and given the name Nugi Garimara. At the age of four she was taken, along

Doris Pilkington.

with her mother and two-year-old sister, Annabelle, to the Moore River Native Settlement. This meant that Doris would never see some of her relatives again, especially her beloved grandmother, Bambaru Banaka. This blind old woman had used the young Doris as her eyes when she went hunting. Instead, Doris grew up at the

Moore River Native Settlement and has said that it never felt like home. She didn't feel like she had found that until she returned to Jigalong over two decades after she left it.

Doris admits to having anger for a long time towards the missionaries who had raised her to believe that Aboriginal people were dirty and evil and who effectively alienated her from her family. She had been told that her mother didn't love her and didn't want her after Molly had again escaped and made the journey home, this time carrying the two-year-old Annabelle. These messages became ingrained and Doris came to believe them. This added to her sense of dislocation.

Again, I can see the resonance with my father's story. Brought up in a boys' home, he was taught that Aboriginal people were savage. He told me how in class it would make him cringe and feel embarrassed. And it was a hard indoctrination to shake. He would, eventually, immerse himself in his Aboriginal culture and embrace it. It would give him pride. But it was a long, long journey to get there. It is just another way in which the story Doris tells about Molly's long journey home is one that many Aboriginal people relate to.

Doris's own journey to get back home was a long, circuitous one. She became a nursing aide, a wife and mother to six children. She would go back to school as a mature-aged student, study journalism, work in film and video and eventually win the David Unaipon award for her first book, *Caprice: A Stockman's Daughter*.

Like my father, Doris found a kind of closure to what had happened to her as a child and to how she felt about herself when she made the journey home to her own family in Jigalong where she had been taken, so many years before. And it was when she returned home and was reunited with her mother that she finally let go of the messages she had been given that her culture was savage and, instead, embraced it. She learnt her traditional language in the hope that she would be able to speak with the older people.

My father did the same. He recorded language and stories and oral histories and family trees. It was as though he needed to record his culture once he found his way back to it. My father's mother had passed away when he was young. Doris, however, had to reconcile the joy of homecoming with painful questions. Why it was she, and not her younger sister Annabelle, who had been left behind? Why was she the one who was abandoned at the age of four-and-a-half, not to see her mother again until twenty-one years later?

Doris would also meet her father who, it turned out, was an Aboriginal man. Doris had assumed that he was white. She recalls that he taught her patience and told her, 'You never be in a hurry, girl. Just sit and wait. You have a cup of tea; you sit there and enjoy it. You enjoy the conversation that's going around.'

## Not all happy endings

It was not all happy endings. Doris would see her younger sister years later when she was working at Perth Hospital. But Annabelle did not want to acknowledge her Aboriginal heritage, her mother or sister. That did not stop Molly from continually hoping that one day her youngest daughter would return.

I often think about Annabelle when I am meditating on *Rabbit-Proof Fence*. Her story is a reminder that, for all of those journeys home, there are so many others who never take that road. Perhaps they never shake the shame they have been brought up to feel about their own cultural heritage. Maybe they have found a home somewhere else or have mentally drawn a line between their past and their present.

And I think of how, when leaving the settlement, Molly had to choose between taking Annabelle or taking Doris. She chose to take her youngest daughter but, as life's course would take it, Annabelle would be the one who eventually abandoned her mother. It was Doris who would return to the fold. And I also think of Molly who, until the end of her life, was waiting for a daughter to return home. It reminds me of my father's uncle, always hoping his sister might come back but passing away three months before Dad finally knocked on his door.

Doris thought that the cruellest thing she ever did was to accuse her mother of giving her away. Said in anger and deeply regretted, she spent much time atoning for it by telling the story of her mother's journey.

I based my novel *Home* on my father's life. It was a fictionalised account of the things I knew about him—he was in an orphanage, he then lived on the streets, he joined the navy, met my mother, married and then had the need to find his family. In writing that novel, by imagining the character in those situations, I felt I came to understand him better than I had before. In a creative sense, I had to walk in his shoes. And so my father also became the inspiration for my second novel, *Legacy*. The story line of this novel was not related to his life the way *Home* was—a fictionalised account that also included many things I knew to be true about his life. Instead, it was a way to explore the emotional relationship I had with him in a completely fictionalised account. It was also my attempt to say that I finally understood why he had the flaws he had. In fact, after all he had been through, it was amazing that he didn't have more. I think of my book as a love letter to him because I wrote it at a point when I felt I had finally come to terms with my relationship with a father who was a difficult, complex man but who I also loved and adored.

So when I see how Doris lovingly crafted her story in *Follow the Rabbit-Proof Fence*, I am reminded again about the deep regret she had for the flash of cruelty she showed to her mother. When I sit down to write, I do it because I want to tell a story but I rarely do it just to entertain. I think most writers are like that. We also write, I believe, to teach, to learn, to heal, to grow, to resolve. These might sound like clichés but they are nonetheless true. And I like to read *Follow the Rabbit-Proof Fence* in the same way, as a love letter to a mother, a way of walking in her shoes.

## Reconnecting

When Doris did eventually reconnect with her family, Molly took her daughter to the wintamarra tree where she was born; I imagine some of the power of that moment as she returned to the very place where she first struggled for life.

Doris came to know more about the circumstances of her separation from her mother and her mother's abandonment of her. Suffering from appendicitis, Molly had been sent to Perth hospital and told she would be able to take her children back home with her when she was better. However, after the operation she and her children were sent to the Moore River Native Settlement as the authorities had no intention of letting the children return to their home. After a while, Molly had again wanted to return home to Jigalong—just as she had done as a child. But she could only carry one child so she was forced to choose, and she chose the younger Annabelle, leaving Doris behind to be cared for by a close relative. Six months later, two-year-old Annabelle would be taken away from Molly.

Over the years, many relatives came to Moore River and they would remind Doris that her mother was Molly Craig from Balfour Downs, near Meekatharra. But it took Doris many years before she could accept her mother's account of what actually happened to her, to change the narrative that had been drummed into her head—that her mother hadn't wanted her. What eventually became clear to Doris is that the authorities had been constantly monitoring her mother, always following her movements. She had been on their radar since her first return from the Moore River Native Settlement as a child.

## Writing our stories

Doris has said that *Follow the Rabbit-Proof Fence* was a book that wouldn't let itself not be written. I can understand why, of all the stories she had to tell about her mother's life, the one about following the rabbit-proof fence to get home would have to be at the heart of her tale. I felt a strong connection to Doris when I read how she was determined to write this book. This aspect of Doris's craft makes sense to me. It touched the writer in me.

When the heart of the next story comes to me, it stays with me. In quiet moments, and sometimes in busy ones, I find myself thinking about the story. I add to it; I subtract from it. I find new twists and new turns. I add layers and peel them back. But always the story is there and it won't leave me until I tell it. People often ask me how I can find time to write. But the story I am working on, the one I have found I need to tell, sits inside my mind and I hear it constantly, like a noisy parrot on my shoulder and it won't shut up until I write down what it is saying.

When I hear the stories about how Doris worked on this book, with more barriers and reasons to stop or delay than I have in my life, I think I understand what it is that drove her to write this story. I am also mindful that Doris sitting down to write a story is a much more ambitious enterprise than anything I have done, one with many more hurdles, one requiring much more determination. She had to fight so much longer and harder. For Doris' generation, the sort of education that I had—graduating first from an Australian university and then from Harvard Law School—was unimaginable. It would have been ambitious for her to just have had thoughts of finishing high school.

I often also think of Doris so meticulously researching her story, using the skills that she eventually went to university to learn, knowing it was the quintessential tale to speak across generations and cultures about the cruelty, impact and legacy of the policy of removing Aboriginal children from their families. I think of how insular and introverted the atmosphere is in libraries —even more so in archives—where you breathe in the dust and the smell of slow-rotting paper. There are so many clues to the stolen lives of Aboriginal people in those archives. This is where my father found my grandmother's removal policy document— the piece of official paper that told him who his family was and where they were from. Doris found pieces of her puzzle there too. Like me, she fleshed out a story based on the stories that her parent told her.

Doris tells of the difficulties she encountered in crafting a story from fragments of snippets in her introduction to *Follow the Rabbit-Proof Fence*. These include the time lapse between when she wrote her book and when the events actually occurred. Memories are not always correct and are sometimes incomplete. Two people can remember the one event very differently. Doris allowed for 'patches of dimmed memories and sketchy reflections'. She had to bear in mind cultural differences—time, numbers and distances don't have the same meanings for traditional Aboriginal people who may remember the season or the aspects of the physical landscape rather than dates, facts and figures. Doris explains that part of her creative practice as a writer was to 'synthesise these different forms of knowledge to give readers the fullest insights into this historic journey'.

Unlike me, however, Doris would not let anyone look at her drafts and nor did she keep them as she perfected her story. She was methodical in her research and determined to get her story absolutely right.

Doris started with the story of her mother's life. Her writer's instinct told her that the story of following the rabbit-proof fence to get home was a powerful allegory for the stolen generations. She had no agenda in telling it. She was not an advocate or an activist back then—though she would speak out on issues later. She was an extraordinary woman with an extraordinary gift for storytelling and an ear and heart for an extraordinary story. This was her primary motivation in writing her book. But the thing about any story—whether book or movie, fact or fiction—is that other people will often have a critical view about what to make of the story. And indeed, it is the role of the audience to interpret the material before them. To digest it. To ponder.

# III

## A STORY THAT HAD TO BE TOLD

One of the links in the chain of events—from Doris penning the story of her mother's life to its debut on the big screen—is the way that once some people heard the story, they simply knew that it really *had* to be told. Like Doris, they were determined to make the movie that would tell it. One of those people—so critical in the chain from book to film—was writer Christine Olsen who would eventually co-produce and write the screenplay.

When I first met Christine Olsen, I fell immediately in love with her. Petite and curly haired, she was a captivating blend of vivacious Meg Ryan and entrancing Diane Keaton. Full of energy, she was intoxicating. I knew instantly that if Christine decided that a film should be made, it would get made. And if she thought a particular director was the right person to make that movie, she would make sure he or she came on board.

The seed for a story can come from anywhere. Sometimes it comes as flashes of ideas and events that then come together. Or it appears as a simple story that turns out to be the skeleton of something larger. And sometimes we meet a character, hear their voice, and the rest of the story follows. If they're like me, some writers keep a journal to capture thoughts, ideas and conversations. We clip items from newspapers or magazines because they strike a chord. Sometimes nothing ignites while at other times there is a slow burn before it ignites into the next project that becomes an all-consuming firestorm.

Christine Olsen.

Christine found that first spark for her screenplay in a review of Doris's book that she read in the newspaper. She clipped it and put it in her folder of ideas for possible future movies. She then read the book and immediately visualised it. With experience of directing, producing and writing (though not of writing a feature length screenplay), she had a well-honed sense of what would work well on the screen in a dramatic, visual telling. Six months later she determined to buy the film rights.

But she wasn't the only one. Learning of other interest, Christine felt that if only she could meet Doris and personally put her case, Doris would be able to see that she, Christine, was the person to whom she could entrust her book. So Christine approached the publishers and a meeting was set up for a trip Doris was to make to Sydney. The meeting was cancelled but, utterly determined, Christine grabbed the opportunity to drive Doris to the airport on her way home. It doesn't surprise me that she convinced Doris she was the right person for the job.

## From book to film

Christine was as careful with her craft as Doris had been. This was no bash-it-out effort. It took five years of research and of writing and rewriting before she was happy with what she had. Along the way she made several trips to Jigalong, the depot on the fence where the girls were taken from their families, and on one visit she stayed with Molly, getting to know the older version of the girl she was bringing to life in her screenplay. Like Doris before her, she knew the story *had* to be told.

Adaptation from book to movie is a deft skill. In a book, a writer can weave the story over long periods of time, have it slowly unfold, knowing that their readers may come into the story, read for a short time, and then return later. They may read over days or weeks, when there is time. With a film, however, the audience has to be fully engaged for the couple of hours that they are in the cinema. In Christine Olsen's screenplay, much is stripped from the book, but she lost none of the story's heart and poignancy.

As the screenplay took shape, Christine decided that the person to direct the movie was Phillip Noyce. She had no fall-back position, no Plan B. I asked her why she wanted him to make the film and she said it was because she knew that if he was involved, it would get made. She also said that, because of his first feature film, *Backroads* (1977)—a film about a couple of criminal drifters, one of whom is Aboriginal—she knew he was able to work with Aboriginal actors and tell stories with Aboriginal characters with authenticity and sensitivity.

And how did she approach Noyce? I expected a tale of many meetings, agents, pitches and negotiations. Instead, Christine found a phone number for Noyce and simply rang it. He was in Hollywood and it was 3:30 in the morning. Noyce recalled:

3:30 AM... October 1999. Fast asleep at my home in the Hollywood hills of Los Angeles. A deep and contented sleep. Deep because post-production on *The Bone Collector* is finally over and already early pre-production has started on *The Sum of All Fears*. Contented because I'm being paid millions of dollars to direct Hollywood blockbusters, featuring stars that will guarantee a gigantic first weekend box office and further inflate my market value as a director. Life couldn't be better.

Then the phone rings. The phone number that nobody except my agent, studio heads and immediate family have access to. At this hour it must be trouble. Big trouble—it's a scriptwriter. An Australian woman who has confused the time difference, tells me something one hears almost every day in Hollywood, 'I've written the perfect script and you're the perfect director for my story'. Gently, I encourage her to call my office during daylight. I immediately leave a message for my assistant, warning him not to encourage her and to announce that I've had to leave hurriedly for New York.

Three months later, after three employees have pleaded with me to read the manuscript that the mysterious caller had sent, I finally relent. I had become such a part of the 'machine' that I'm convinced nothing worthwhile could possibly reach my desk except through the Hollywood filtering process of studio executives and agents. Worse, the dawn caller (or the crazy lady as I've now christened her) has never written a screenplay before. Her name is Christine Olsen...[3]

Christine remembers Noyce as polite but firm. She is certain he thought she was crazy. She forwarded her screenplay which was first read by Noyce's business partner, Kathleen McLaughlin, who became convinced that this story *had* to be filmed, and that Noyce was the one to film it.

## The right director

Noyce is a country boy, son of a solicitor, from Griffith in rural New South Wales. This is a part of Australia with an active Italian community, not simply a place filled with middle-class white Australians. Noyce is one of the most successful Australian directors having made a huge career for himself in Hollywood. But he learnt his craft at film school and by making documentaries and low-budget movies in Australia before going on to make big-budget action-thrillers such as *Dead Calm, Patriot Games, The Bone Collector, Salt* and *The Quiet American*.

With this international, mainstream success it is easy to forget that he has the understanding of an outsider towards mainstream Australian cinema that often borrows from Hollywood. That understanding is evident in *Backroads*, Noyce's first feature film, and convinced Olsen he was the right director for her project.

*Backroads* is, as the title implies, a road movie. Based on a short story by Josephine Emery (as John Emery), it tells the story of Gary, a young Aboriginal man played by the charismatic Gary Foley, and Jack, an older, racist white man, played by one of Australia's favourite actors, Bill Hunter. They steal a car and drive through rural New South Wales, heading towards the coast. On their journey they steal guns, alcohol and anything else they need. They visit several Aboriginal communities and meet a range of characters, Indigenous and non-

Indigenous. After they commit murder, they are chased by the police and arrested. Gary is shot when he tries to escape.

Casting Foley was a bold but smart decision. A hot-blooded and articulate Indigenous activist who until then had never acted on film before, Noyce described Foley as 'a handsome

Phillip Noyce.

firebrand with matinee idol looks'. (I would still describe him this way.)[4] Noyce tells how he approached Foley for the part:

> I was told to ring Gary at a pub in the Aboriginal ghetto of Redfern [Sydney] called the Cricketer's Arms. I rang and went over to this pub full of Aborigines and told Gary that I wanted him to be a movie star. And Gary said he didn't want any part of white man's bullshit unless he got to monitor all of the black content. So we reached this agreement that he could rewrite his dialogue whenever he thought it was bullshit; he could have a say in the movie's content.[5]

Noyce understood that Foley knew infinitely more about the experiences of black people than he did. Noyce knew he could not make his film unless he was faithful to the Aboriginal perspective that Foley could bring. He also knew he couldn't make the movie without access to the small Aboriginal communities that Foley could walk into. So Noyce blended Foley's own experiences into the film's narrative. Foley's stamp on the movie is clear and this process of actively incorporating an Aboriginal perspective was a democratic style of filmmaking that was rare in the Australian movie industry.

Foley writes that Noyce sought his assistance to film in Bourke and Brewarrina, towns in northwest New South Wales with complex histories of race relations. They were places where, as Foley writes, 'the Koori community generally were wary of Anglo-Australia film producers and directors making films that usually portrayed Kooris in negative ways'. That Foley got the communities of Bourke and Brewarrina to collaborate with him is a testament to his high standing with them. As Foley states on his website, *Backroads* is an

> historic film in terms of being the first film featuring Aboriginal people where Aboriginal people had a significant say in the making of the film. In both the manner in which they were portrayed and also whether they even wanted the film made in their midst. It was the first Australian film where the only people paid award wages were the local Indigenous actors and extras, because the entire budget for the film was $25,000.[6]

The democratic filmmaking style helped Noyce make a better movie than it would otherwise have been. He credits Foley with a much better ending—one true to real life—than originally planned. Initially, the final scene had the men abandon their car on the Sydney Harbour Bridge and head to the city. Gary, however, thought the film should end tragically and realistically, with Gary being killed as he tries to escape from the police. In an act that acknowledges Foley's central role in the making of the film, Noyce eventually signed the rights of *Backroads* over to him.

One can easily see the flaws in *Backroads* which even Noyce acknowledges, noting the handicap he faced in raising enough funding to even complete this very low-budget movie. But its strengths can't be ignored either. *Backroads* is a brave film and a confronting one. As the German film scholar Ingo Petzke observes, it was the first Australian film to accuse Australians of deeply ingrained racism and it did so in a very graphic way. It shows an Aboriginal experience of a people who had reached a degree of apathy because they were continually told there was no use striking out, that they just had to accept things the way they were. And when they did strike out, there were inevitable, inescapable, tragic consequences. These are not cheerful themes and the movie offers no false hope. All this helps explain why Olsen was so convinced that Noyce was the right director for her screenplay.[7]

Noyce learned a lot of lessons while making *Backroads* and he remembered these decades later when he was making *Rabbit-Proof Fence*. In his own words:

> The two stories are set just 45 years apart, but they are in reality separated by 150 years. One deals with indigenous characters on the eastern seaboard of Australia, where contact started to take place from 1778 with the establishment of the first penal colony, and where by the 1970s Aboriginal culture was almost at its lowest point, almost utterly decimated. Whereas *Rabbit-Proof Fence* is set in the Western Australian desert in the last areas settled by white people. Back in 1931, and even today, Aboriginal people in this area have managed to cling to some

of their traditional lifestyle and certainly have managed to maintain spiritual connections to their traditional lands. So, the films are very different. One is about hopelessness and the other is about hope, hope being much more possible where the Aboriginal people have managed to cling to just a little bit of what they had when Europeans first came to Australia.[8]

Petzke notes that the two films act as a set of brackets around Noyce's Australian work. Different as they are in content and intention, they are both based on one of the concepts most inextricably linked to Australian identity: being on the road. I agree: *Rabbit-Proof Fence* seems like a road movie to me—just one without a car, or even a proper road.

## Noyce's own journey home

At the time he read Olsen's script, Noyce was getting ready to make the $104 million budget Hollywood movie, *The Sum of All Fears*. In his diary he records: 'ten pages into the [*Rabbit-Proof Fence*] screenplay... I find myself crying.' He kept thinking about the story of three Aboriginal girls walking home and their desire to get back to their homeland and to their mothers. The story captivated him in the same way it had captivated Doris Pilkington, Christine Olsen and the three members of his company who had urged him to read the screenplay:

It was the kind of story that kept coming back to me over the following months, as if I was drawn by an invisible voice. A voice, I later realised, that was telling me to follow the lead of young Molly and make the journey home myself.[9]

Noyce also felt the story was about himself:

> As I read, those children quickly become my children and strangely I become a child again, yearning to find the Rabbit-Proof Fence that bi-sects the Australian continent and just might be the way back home. For me and for them. After ten years in Hollywood, I'm still an outsider, a migrant guest worker telling other people's stories. As a citizen of the world, without nationality, I've become the ultimate Hollywood foot soldier, directing action/adventure, escapist stories designed to mesmerise across all boundaries. I know that black-themed films have never worked at the Australian Cinema box office. But it's time to go home.[10]

Frustrated with navigating the Hollywood system of big budgets, Noyce walked away from *The Sum of All Fears* which he'd promised then Paramount chief Sherry Lansing he'd direct.[11] He got in a taxi, went to the airport, boarded a plane, came back to Australia and started preparing for *Rabbit-Proof Fence* with a handycam.

Noyce had been making big-star, huge budget movies for years but this story about three little Aboriginal girls wouldn't let go of him. This was a film that would also take him on a journey. He was attracted to a story for which he was told he could never raise the funding in Australia because Australians didn't want to see films about Aboriginal people, that he would never sell overseas because non-Australians wouldn't be interested either, and for which he would never be able to find the young Aboriginal girls to play the three leading roles. Every time he was told he would never be able to do it, he became more determined.

Everlyn Sampi as Molly and Tianna Sansbury as Daisy.

# IV

## A FILM THAT HAD TO BE MADE

When Phil Noyce committed to *Rabbit-Proof Fence*, like Christine he did his research. He met with Doris, visited Moore River and followed the fence all the way to Jigalong. In an air-conditioned four-wheel drive, in three days he traversed the distance that the girls took nine weeks to travel by foot. In Jigalong, he met the real Molly who was now 86, and the real Daisy, now 79. He then had to find the right actors to play them and their cousin, Gracie, as little girls.

A lot goes into pulling together the cast and crew for a movie. It is not just the enormity of the task of booking everyone from the caterers and make-up artists to the designers, cinematographers, editors, sound crew and actors for a big budget film. It is also making sure that every decision helps create the look and feel of the story. Each is a step in the foundation of the director's storytelling craft.

### Finding the right three girls

Noyce always knew that the success of his film would be dependent on finding the right three girls to play the leading parts. And he was told from the start that he would not be able

Laura Monaghan as Gracie and Tianna Sansbury as Daisy.

to find three Aboriginal children who could act. There are no well-known professional Aboriginal child actors in Australia—in part because there is so little demand for them from mainstream film and television. Noyce was not daunted by the challenge of casting and was optimistic about his chances. He said later that he thought of the history of performance that is an integral part of Aboriginal oral culture where history is told by telling stories, handed down from generation to generation. So he knew there was a rich potential. He just had to mine for it. To find the right three girls he knew he was just going to have to look in every corner of the country.

And travel the country he did. Crossing the continent, sometimes in four-wheel drives and helicopters, he and his casting team, led by Christine King, considered over two thousand children of whom Noyce met over eight hundred personally. He started by looking in cities and towns but came to realise fairly quickly that he needed to look in remoter areas for children who knew more about traditional lifestyle because in the movie they would be playing Aboriginal children who had only recently come into contact with white culture. He needed children who lacked worldliness.

Since experience was not going to be a criteria in his prospective stars, Noyce had to look for children who had an 'it' factor, an on-screen charisma. He needed his actors to have imagination, and also to be able to handle the pressure-cooker atmosphere of a movie set and to concentrate for long periods of time. He described the challenge of casting as having to find three girls who were readily identifiable as Aboriginal but to whom the rest of Australia—and indeed the world—would feel they could connect.

Darlene Johnson's documentary, *Following the Rabbit-Proof Fence*, is a behind-the-scenes look at the making of the movie that shows Noyce involved in the process of casting. He is shown walking around a boisterous school sports carnivals, auditioning children and then, as he starts to narrow down the possible candidates, working with them in workshops to see their potential, measuring each child's talent and on-screen charisma and exploring the dynamics between the girls. Throughout, Noyce is like an enthusiastic grandfather. In what must have been a complex, exhausting and daunting process, he is having an enormous amount of fun and is genuinely enjoying his interactions with the children.

Assisting Noyce from the start was Rachael Maza, a well-known Aboriginal actress from her many television performances and having had a starring role in Rachel Perkin's film, *Radiance*. Noyce knew his young actors would need someone who understood their culture and who could provide them professional and emotional support. He also knew that culturally, since he was casting three girls, this close assistance should come from a woman. In Darlene's documentary, Rachael is shown constantly with the girls, coaching and coaxing, their protector, instructor and friend.

Noyce has said that, during the casting, he felt like he was digging for gold:

> There you are, chipping away at this mountain with mostly failure day after day, and yet, like any prospector I was fuelled by the knowledge—and perhaps optimism—that somewhere you are going to find a nugget. In fact, I did better than that; I found three diamonds, perfectly cut.[12]

Everlyn Sampi as Molly, Tianna Sansbury as Daisy and Laura Monaghan as Gracie.

The diamonds were Everlyn Sampi as Molly, Laura Monaghan as Gracie and Tianna Sansbury as Daisy.

At just eleven years of age, Everlyn was the eldest and she was also the one who for Noyce stood out from all the hundreds of children who he met and interviewed. Everyln lived in the Aboriginal community of Djarindjin in northern Western Australia. The policy of removing Aboriginal children had touched Evelyn's life: her mother, Glenys Sampi, was four years old when she was taken to a mission to be brought up by nuns and would not be reunited with her mother for ten years.

In her audition tape, Everlyn says that she likes fishing and camping. She comes across as shy but, with her long plaited hair, she also seems to have a determination, a strength. She has a natural beauty and, even though she does not look directly at the camera, she catches it and the camera loves her. Noyce saw this refusal to look at him was a cultural practice, that Aboriginal people often avoided eye contact as a sign of respect. When Noyce decided that she was right for Molly he began casting the other characters around her.

Laura Monaghan, a young girl from Port Hedland in Western Australia, was cast in the role of Gracie. Noyce was attracted to her intelligence, dignity and charm. She had the same mix of quiet strength but endearing vulnerability that he was looking for in all his leads. Noyce knew this mix was crucial because these were all highly vulnerable children who needed the strength to survive the whole experience. Laura had huge potential. In the workshops she is charismatic and photogenic. Lastly, Noyce cast the role of Daisy, the youngest character. But just two weeks before filming was to start, he decided that she wouldn't cope with the process of making the movie, that he couldn't put this particular young girl through it.

I admire this about Noyce. It was difficult finding the actresses for his key parts and, finally, he had them. He knew his movie depended on them, on his ability to cast these roles properly. But, if he suspected that doing the movie wasn't the right thing for any of the actresses, then he wouldn't exploit them, even if it meant that the movie wouldn't get made. It was just another indication that Christine Olsen's instinct about Noyce being the right director for this film was absolutely correct.

Noyce looked back through his casting notes and remembered a young girl who had auditioned as an extra, Tianna Sansbury. The audition at which Tianna made such an impression is captured in Darlene Johnson's documentary. Noyce asks the girls to come into the room and tell him that there are some kids outside who are in trouble. They then have to try to persuade him to go with them and help sort out the problem. Tianna is so convincing that Noyce later said he thought for a second that there really was some problem outside. Tianna's family had, like Everlyn's, also been touched by the policy of removing Aboriginal children: both her mother and aunt had been taken away as children because they were half-caste.

Tianna is a beautiful, wide-eyed child and as an actress she has a natural, pure talent and a gentle defiance. After being cast in the role of Daisy just six days before filming began, she turned out to be extraordinary. Noyce says that he has to fall in love with the actresses in his movies in the way he hopes the audience will and it is easy to see from her audition how most people would instantly fall in love with Tianna. Noyce must have thought he'd hit the jackpot—and been very relieved.

As the start date for shooting drew closer and the pressure on her drew greater, Everlyn became unsettled. She ran away just four days before shooting began but she came back. Noyce seemed to understand that Everlyn's unsettledness was not a sign of a lack of commitment; it was a sign of a lack of self-assurance. She was a child doing an adult's job. He worked hard to build Everlyn's confidence—and Rachael Maza did, too. Everlyn was precocious, vivacious but wilful. Noyce had to be careful and manage her insecurity. At times he must have wondered whether the whole task was too much. But his patience paid off and Everlyn became not just a natural actress but a natural leader. Noyce has compared her to other actresses who had starred in his movies—to Nicole Kidman and Angelina Jolie.

As Noyce knew would be the case, at the end of casting his three lead roles, he had three actresses from a very different cultural background to his, all with a very limited experience of the world who had never acted before. But he also had three children unaffected by acting training and who had natural instincts. They already had the energy that was needed, he just needed to help them harness it and he continued to rely on Rachael Maza to prepare them technically and emotionally. Noyce was able to get the best from his three young actresses by gradually getting them used to the cameras and an ever-expanding crew. Their families—including cousins—were brought to the sets so the girls would not get homesick.

The three leading actresses might not have had any acting experience but they already knew the worlds of the characters and Noyce just had to elicit these worlds from them. He said that Everlyn had all the characteristics of the real Molly and he had to get her in touch with her natural instincts; that was all she needed to make the part work. He used their lack of acting experience to his advantage and described this process of working with his stars on *Rabbit-Proof Fence* as the opposite to how he would have approached it in Hollywood. It is not unlike the way he had trusted Gary Foley, all those years ago in *Backroads,* to bring his own experiences to the film, to let the Aboriginal voice shape his story.

## Casting decisions

There are many noteworthy Australian actors in *Rabbit-Proof Fence*: David Gulpilil, Deborah Mailman, Ningali Lawford, Garry McDonald and Jason Clarke. But one of the most important casting decisions was of that of the charismatic Northern Irish actor Kenneth Branagh as the Chief Protector, A.O. Neville, whose job it had been to administer the legislation that controlled Aboriginal people, including the policy of removing Aboriginal children from their parents.

Branagh is a Shakespearean actor whose films include *Hamlet* and *Henry V* but who has also played roles in films as varied as *Harry Potter and the Chamber of Secrets*, *The Boat that Rocked* and *My Week with Marilyn*. He responded overnight to the script after he received it, and then prepared at length by researching the role. A world-class veteran of stage and screen, a director as well as an actor, it is not surprising that he developed strong ideas about how to shape the character of A.O. Neville to both heighten the drama and draw out the themes of this film.

Branagh saw Neville as a man who had admiration for Aboriginal people but who led a program that had a profoundly negative effect. He said that he liked the way the film tried 'to neither judge Neville nor to excuse him and that is what was interesting about the part'. He wanted to portray him as human. Noyce also sees benevolence with devastating consequences in A.O. Neville: 'Nothing can be more terrifying than a man who really believes that what he is doing is right—who kills with his kindness.' [13] Noyce found that Branagh's characterisation of Neville exceeded his expectations: 'He was able to bring a complex humanity to a character that could easily have become a caricature of evil.'

In an insightful series of observations about what the fictionalised character of A.O. Neville would and should stand for in order to increase the power of the story, Branagh wrote of his interpretation of the complicated role that the Chief Protecter played in history:

Kenneth Branagh as A.O. Neville, Everlyn Sampi as Molly and Kate Roberts as Matron.

He seemed to spend much of his professional life under siege. Often a political scapegoat. Constantly under-funded, his policies constantly challenged (he might say undermined) and continually having to justify his actions and in so doing often masking his genuine fascination with the Native culture. He loved the country and the people, and yet had through his empire background a paternalistic, often ruthless attitude, towards a race that he also had a tremendous compassion for. I feel that the more extremely we can see these contradictory forces in him, the better. A man torn between what is ideal,

what is necessary and what is possible. If we can see his shock
at their treatment, his admiration for the full bloods, his deep
concern for the young girls, we should more powerfully feel
the intense force of his vision. His dangerously flawed vision.
A subtitle for his role in the film could be 'Neville in Crisis'.[14]

Drama is about conflict. And I am interested in Branagh's
intuitive ability to find the key conflicts in the character he played.
He understood the dramatic importance of making Neville a
metaphor for a broader community struggle and the ideological
battles of the time while making sure that he was not simply an
evil caricature. Neville had to have some humanity. Branagh's
observations explain to some extent how an historical figure
like Neville becomes subjected to dramatic interpretation. He is
used not simply as a character but also to portray a set of ideals.

## Image and sound

Shooting began in September 2000 on location in the barren
landscape of the Flinders Ranges in South Australia. Shooting
on location is challenging. It is costly to accommodate and feed
the crew. There is the harshness and unpredictability of the
weather. The look of the movie, its sweeping scenes and its use
of the landscape as an additional character in the film, are largely
attributable to Noyce's choice of Christopher Doyle as the Director
of Photography.

As a cinematographer for a film set in outback Australia, Doyle
may have seemed an odd choice. Although Australian born, he
had worked extensively in Asian art house cinema and often
shot in confined spaces. But he was skilled at using a hand-held
camera and Noyce felt that this would be an advantage in giving

an earthiness to the scenes, shooting in such remote locations but also in capturing his child actors who had not been trained to work with a camera. A still camera, according to Doyle, loses the rawness while the flexibility of the handheld camera allows for the creation of a particular energy. It also allowed him to capture the young actresses responses to situations without the need for further takes.

Doyle was drawn to the project because he wanted to work with Noyce, was interested to finally make his first movie in Australia, and because he was drawn to a 'road movie on foot'. For Doyle, *Rabbit-Proof Fence* was a new challenge: it was rural and remote landscapes rather than the cityscapes he was used to. And he captures beautifully the physical demands of the journey, the loneliness in such vastness and the isolation and remoteness of the space. One striking aspect of the Australian outback is the wide skies—the vast blueness. And I like the dark look that Chris Doyle gives the film. Molly, Daisy and Gracie were running from the authorities and taking a dangerous path. They were not in blue-sky times. The bleakness is captured in the tones and hues of the film. Doyle appreciated this and he gave the film that feel deliberately.

While this movie is so much about the landscape, it is brought together by its soundscape. World-renown musician Peter Gabriel crafted a hypnotic and emotional musical accompaniment to the movie that resonates with its soul. On hearing it, I think of the work of my favourite Aboriginal composer, David Page, and I can visualise Bangarra dancers interpreting the nuance of each note. The layering of sound has always been Gabriel's strength.

Gabriel initially met with Noyce to discuss doing the soundtrack to what would be Noyce's next film, a big-budget Miramax remake of the Graham Greene story, *The Quiet American*.[15] On impulse, Noyce mentioned *Rabbit-Proof Fence* explaining that, unlike the Hollywood movie, there was no budget for a composer on the Australian film. Gabriel came back to Noyce to say he would work on *Rabbit-Proof Fence*.

Gabriel had received plenty of offers to work on film soundtracks after he worked on Martin Scorsese's *The Last Temptation of Christ* in 1986. He had been reluctant to accept them because his process was slow and he always had other projects. But *Rabbit-Proof Fence* attracted him because he liked the independent nature of the film and the power and simplicity of the film. He also felt that this would be a story with strong atmosphere and mood, not a lot of dialogue, and so the music would play a major role in telling it. Gabriel was one more person drawn in by the power of the story of three Aboriginal girls crossing the desert on foot to find their way home.

Gabriel is well-known as the founding member of Genesis and for his successful solo career. Perhaps less known is his extensive work as a groundbreaker in the incorporation and promotion of world music. He has also been active in human rights organisations such as Amnesty International and Greenpeace. It is easy to see why this story would have drawn him.

Gabriel's layered, intuitive music is one of the strengths of the film. I have long loved his rich style and I have a particular fondness for songs such as 'In Your Eyes', 'Red Rain' and 'Don't Give Up' which had formed part of the soundtrack to my own life as important relationships blossomed or faltered. His work on *Rabbit-Proof Fence*, particularly 'Stealing the Children', 'Gracie's recapture', and 'The Return Parts 1, 2, and 3', has the same ability to hit the right emotional strings.

*Rabbit-Proof Fence* was set in the 1930s but the period was not going to be evoked by simply using songs from that era. Gabriel wanted to make music that 'came out of the earth'. Using contemporary music wouldn't work—he wanted to build the soundtrack up using the natural sounds that would have been recorded. He knew that there were not a lot of man-made noises around when the girls walked along the rabbit-proof fence.

The music weaves seamlessly throughout the movie. Gabriel responded to scenes he saw but for something that knits so well with the movie, it is remarkable that he did his work on the movie remotely. But distance is no barrier to close collaboration today. The sound team would send sounds of the bush they had recorded—bird song, wind, rain—and Gabriel would work on them in his studio in the United Kingdom. MP3 files would go back and forth on email as Gabriel's team worked on orchestrating the musical score. Noyce would later say that, despite the fact that they were geographically far away, it was one of the closest collaborations he'd ever had with a composer on a film.

Many working on the film said they became close; there were no black-white frictions on the set the way there had been when Noyce made *Backroads*. Doris, a script consultant with a title credit as a writer, was proactive in providing feedback for the script. There was, again as in *Backroads*, collaboration and consultation to make sure the script was true to the story it told and that it resonated and was imbued with an Aboriginal perspective and experience. This aspect of the collaboration is a testament to Noyce's working style and sensitivity and to Doris's continual committed, determined proprietorship over her own story.

Doris was right to entrust Christine with her story; and Christine had been right to take the story to Noyce.

# V

## STOLEN FROM HOME

When watching *Rabbit-Proof Fence* the first time, the story swept me along. But now, every time I see it, I look at it more forensically and I find something else to like about the images, words, sounds. For a movie that has a sparse script, there is a lot to say about it. And for me, each scene matters.

### A clash of cultures

*Rabbit-Proof Fence* is a story about two worlds and a clash of cultures. The world of white Australia for Aboriginal people is set up quickly with blunt words in cold text on a couple of captions:

Western Australia 1931.
For 100 years, the Aboriginal Peoples have resisted the
invasion of their lands by white settlers.

Now, a special law, the Aborigines Act,
controls their lives in every detail.

Mr A.O. Neville, the Chief Protector of Aborigines,
is the legal guardian of every Aborigine in the
State of Western Australia.

He has the power
'to remove any half-caste child' from their family,
from anywhere within the state.

And so we first meet the antagonist—Mr A.O. Neville—and in him we have a villain wielding a repressive law that controls the lives of a colonised people. We also know that we have a story with a perspective and a political point of view. Noyce uses the charged language of 'invasion', reflective much more of an Aboriginal interpretation of history than that of the coloniser.

In stark contrast, we then cut the hypnotic beauty of the desert landscape filmed from an aeroplane. And although we don't yet know it—there are no English subtitles—we hear the sound of Molly Craig—the real Molly Craig—talking in her language, Martu Wangka, a Western Desert Language. She is telling us about Gracie and Daisy, and about her life and family at Jigalong.

If I ever needed to explain how Aboriginal art can be a topographic map, I would simply show this opening shot of *Rabbit-Proof Fence*. It immediately sets up a sense of place. We see the beauty of this remote world and I for one want to be there. The film shows it as a place of home, of familiarity, of happiness and safety. And we already know this when, played by Everlyn, Molly first appears on our screen as a young girl.

From the very start, then, the film juxtaposes the laws and policies of politicians and bureaucrats with the real lives of the Aboriginal people affected by them—the richness of their culture and the strength of their connection to family and land little understood by the decision-makers. We have been introduced to two cultures, two different worldviews. We have also been introduced to Molly and we know this is her story. She has the perfect mix of strength and vulnerability. There is laughter in her eyes and a slight smile on her lips. As she looks to the sky, she is curious about the world around her.

## Happy in her world

Molly is happy in her world. She is told by her mother, Maude (Ningali Lawford), that the eagle is her spirit bird and that it will look after her. And we see the older women, including Molly's mother and grandmother (Myarn Lawford) with the young girls, Molly, Daisy and Gracie, hunting a goanna. The girls are learning bush craft, learning to track, learning to find food. When Molly spies a goanna, she rushes to pull it from the tree. She is confident and fearless, a girl of action.

There is an intruder in this world. We first see the boot of Constable Riggs (Jason Clarke) before we meet him. He is the Local Protector and, while the women are not aware of his presence, he is watching and monitoring them. Already we sense his control. The boot represents his authority and power and indicates a cultural difference as the women are bare footed. The camera tilts upwards and we see his rifle. This not only reinforces his power, it makes him menacing and he embodies the danger, the threat, his position poses to Molly and her world.

Lurking in the trees with Constable Riggs is the Depot Manager, Hungerford (Andrew S. Gilbert), who runs the store at the Aboriginal community of Jigalong. Hungerford identifies Molly, Gracie and Daisy as half-castes whose fathers are not around. Their tone is not comforting; there is a sense of danger and vulnerability. Hungerford is no ally of the Aboriginal people he works with but simply another authority figure, tasked with regulating and controlling.

When the women finally sense Constable Riggs is present, Maude tells Molly to hide the children. They have been taught that the police are dangerous and they know that they are vulnerable. This scene haunts me. It clearly evokes the terror a parent must have felt, living in the shadow of the fear that their children would be taken away. It reminds me of the stories I heard as a child of what people had done to keep their children hidden during the era when they were removed. I remember my father telling me about one woman who travelled between towns carrying her child in a suitcase. And on the reserves and in the towns, all the children were warned and trained to hide when they saw the police or their cars.

Of course, not all remote Aboriginal communities were as pristine as the way we see Jigalong on the screen. But a cinematic point is being made here. This romanticised, stylised view of camp life is reflective of the internal relationship that the girls have with their home. It is where they are from. It is where they are happy. It reflects the strength of their family relationships. And out in the bush, there was the opportunity for better diets and a healthier way of living.

## The Chief Protector's power

From the world of Molly's family home we move to the world of Mr A.O. Neville in his office in Perth. The difference between the world of Jigalong and the world of the city is symbolic of both their physical distance from each other and the cultural differences. It also symbolises the distance between where Molly and her family live and where the fundamental decisions are made about their lives. We see Neville's power in his determined pose, the diligence in his work. He fills in a card, categorising Molly—fourteen years of age, 'dark but not full blood'. This power he has is evidenced as he makes decisions about whether to exempt someone from the regulations: whether they can marry, whether they can visit their children, whether they can have a new pair of shoes. This is his ordinary, day-to-day business, the kind of decisions that have profound consequences, and which he makes determinedly, efficiently, methodically—and unemotionally. The camera looks up at him, highlighting his power, his place of dominion.

To underline the power he has, the film immediately gives us a glimpse of the impact of those decisions. A mother weeps outside his office building, seeking permission to visit her child. Neville is unmoved. He is more concerned about the report from Riggs about the three half-caste children at Jigalong. He orders their removal, particularly concerned that the youngest is reported as having been promised in marriage. For all the coldness of his decision-making and the failure to be moved by its consequence, we do see that Mr Neville is motivated by the belief that he is saving the girls from a dangerous fate. Whatever value judgements we place on his actions today, Noyce was right to make sure that we saw the ideological impetus behind Neville's actions.

Back at Jigalong, a bell rings. We are back in the imposed rigid, structured life that Neville is trying to implement into the community of Jigalong, a life of rations and everyone knowing their place. The girls talk to a fence builder (Anthony Hayes) who tells them all about the fence. They are fascinated but, unlike the audience, unaware of the role that it will play in their future. As Molly's mother gets her rations we see the same defiance that we will see in her daughter. She answers the Depot Manager's remarks about Molly with a cheeky observation that if Mr Neville, whom she calls 'Mr Devil', wants half-caste kids, he should make his own. Through this banter though, the women's awareness of the control Neville has over their lives is clear. This man in Perth has the power to take their children away and the whole community lives with this fear every day. They use humour to mock authority and to survive.

## Stolen

Then, as a car arrives, the children and mothers sense danger and they run desperately. But the children are chased into the car, herded like animals. The constable points to his papers, the power and authority, ignoring the terror and wailing of the children as they are literally torn from their mothers' arms. This is the most haunting, disturbing scene in the film. It was filmed towards the end of the schedule and in Darlene Johnson's documentary the cast talk about how, at this stage in the filming, the three young girls had felt like family and the emotion on the set was raw. One senses that Jason Clarke, as Riggs, felt it as well. The scene hits a nerve in the cast many of whom had been removed themselves. The wailing is heartbreaking and the sight of the mothers, frantically chasing the car, makes it almost unbearable.

In the lead up to this scene, we have seen the importance of land, home, language and culture to Molly and her extended family. The sounds and images of the pain, the outpouring of grief and emotional carnage that the girls' removal causes is critical in reminding us that, as with all stolen generations stories, the impact on those who lost their children, grandchildren or siblings is as destructive as it was on those who were removed. The film offers an important reminder that the policy did not consider whether children were loved and were cared for. These were insignificant factors in the decision to remove them.

Tianna Sansbury as Daisy, Jason Clarke as Riggs, Ningali Lawford as Maude and
Everlyn Sampi as Molly.

The shot of the girls looking out the back window of the car as it pulls away when they are captured is powerful. It is a metaphor for the last glance at a family and life the children will never see again. This cinematic image resonates strongly with me. As I mentioned earlier, in my novel *Home,* loosely based on the life of my own grandmother, I wrote a fictional account of her being removed from where she lived (Dungalear Station) by the Aboriginal Protection Board. I describe how, after she is captured and put into the police car, ripped away from her brother, she struggles to see out the back window, to get a last look at the brother, camp and life she will never see again. I had not seen *Rabbit-Proof Fence* before I wrote my novel so this scene cuts very close to the bone.

As the wailing and trauma of this act of violence—heightened unbearably by the sound of Gabriel's relentless drumming—fade down, we hear Neville's voice: 'As you know, every Aborigine born in this state comes under my control.' It is a reminder that it was by his order that the girls were removed from their mothers. We see him delivering a lecture to middle-class white women in Perth on his concerns about the 'half-caste' race and their increasing numbers. He explains the policy and the logic behind it in scientific terms, using pictures in his slide show of real families, about the need to regulate marriages and the ability to breed out the race. Over a photograph of Moore River Native Settlement, we are told that the purpose of the policy is to give Aboriginal people the benefits of white culture and to train them for domestic service and farm labour. Neville uses phrases such as 'for their own good', 'unwanted third race', 'advance to white status' and 'in spite of himself, the native must be helped'.

## Good intentions, callous practice

After the high emotion of the preceeding scene, we experience the tension between the good intentions and the reality of implementing a policy which had, at its heart, a callous practice of destroying a race by separating children from their parents. These are the arguments that justify the policy and they are laid out for us just as they were for the white women of Perth. Neville's final sentence about how the Aboriginal people 'must be helped' segues straight to Molly, Gracie and Daisy in a steel cage being taken to the Moore River Native Settlement by train. The windows are barred and we see Molly's face through them as she stares out from her cell. The girls are treated as prisoners or criminals, not children. As the landscape rushes by they are separated from their country not just by the growing distance from their families and home but by the metaphorical cage they have been put in as they head towards an institution that will supposedly assimilate them into white Australian culture. It is a symbolic separation from the cultural practice and family relationships we saw the girls enjoying in the opening sequence.

After the train, the girls get put on the back of a truck, herded and tethered like farm animals as they travel through an ever-changing terrain. The length of the journey, its arduousness and its strangeness to the girls are apparent. When the girls finally arrive at the Settlement, their home at Jigalong is 1200 miles away to the north. The unfamiliarity of this new world to three exhausted and frightened children is shown in the way that they huddle against each other. Little Daisy thinks the Matron (Kate Roberts), all dressed in white, is a ghost.

## Mission life

The girls are introduced to life at the mission and its strict rules—regimented activities, dormitories, no speaking traditional language, sometimes no speaking at all, standing to pray before meals—it offers another deep contrast to the freedom of life in the opening sequence. Nina (Natasha Wanganeen) is the Dormitory Boss of the children—though only a child herself—and she guides Molly, Gracie and Daisy through the routines. Apart from the strict regimes, the thing that also stands in stark contrast to the place they have come from is the lack of love and warmth the girls are shown. They are shouted at, scrubbed and taught to be obedient, by both black and white people.

At an assembly, where Neville attends the Settlement, Nina explains that the lighter skinned girls will be sent to an institution for Aboriginal girls where they are trained to be domestic servants or to work in hospitals. The lighter the skin, supposedly the easier to educate and assimilate. When Molly is called up, Chris Doyle's camera shows us her point of view as she takes the long walk up to the Chief Protector, the slow motion of the shot reflecting and evoking Molly's fear. Neville inspects her, telling her that she will adjust, that she will learn 'duty, service, responsibility'. We see Molly in close-up, her face showing feelings of terror at being examined, weighed up, categorised, and of being separated once again, this time from Daisy and Gracie. Her terror is made evident in a close-up of Neville's face—strange and almost distorted. She understands her fate is in his hands. But he says 'no'—she is too dark. She will stay at Moore River rather than be sent away. And with that, a decision based purely on skin colour, her fate is decided.

As the girls begin to learn the tasks expected of them—sweeping and cleaning in the room with all the babies who had been taken—another young resident, Olive (Tamara Flanagan), is returned after attempting an escape, brought back by Moodoo (David Gulpilil), the Aboriginal tracker. Olive's punishment is a cautionary tale to the others—she is beaten by the Settlement manager, Mr Neal (Garry McDonald), her hair is cut and she is locked in a cell-like room in solitary

Kate Roberts as Matron.

confinement. This is the cost of trying to escape.

I need to pause here and give some thought to the character of Moodoo, the Aboriginal tracker. Why would he be involved in the hunting of escaped children and bringing them back to where they would be punished? Why is he complicit in this assimilation project, in oppressing his own people? In fact, his motivations become clear when we learn that he has a daughter at Moore River and it is this that keeps him tied there. He has also been on some kind of probation and this has just ended. He is free to go, but his daughter is not. He wants to be near her and, more than that, he wants to take her home to the Kimberley. It is evident that this is a vain hope—Neville is clear that the girl will remain—but Moodoo holds on to this dream tenaciously nonetheless.

Molly asks Nina about all the babies in the dormitory. She explains that they have no mothers, that no-one at Moore River has a mother. Molly replies that she does. Nina looks to the

David Gulpilil as Moodoo.

ground: she's heard this many times before but she knows, over time, they all feel abandoned, motherless. Molly, however, has her own interpretation of this world. As she lies in bed, in a dreamlike sequence we see her anger towards the people who now control her life, who threaten the freedom she has known—the tracker, Mr Neville, Constable Riggs, the Matron. 'You make me sick', she chants over and over. It is both a statement of how she feels about them and of the fact that she knows her spirit will be crushed if she stays there, the way Olive's is being broken. We also see her desire to return to her mother and her home, and, through the image of her spirit bird, we know that the connections she has to her land and her culture are unbroken.

## Escape

On their second morning Molly resolves to escape, to walk home. She has seen a storm coming. A tempest, usually a cinematic omen of turmoil and destruction, offers Molly opportunity for the very practical reason that she knows rain can wash away tracks. Gracie is reluctant, fearful, about the plan to escape and Daisy is worried about the tracker. The girls all know the cost of capture—they have seen Olive's fate—but nothing can diminish Molly's desire to get back home. If anything, Olive's treatment has only made her determined to reject the life at Moore River. She takes Daisy and a reluctant Gracie; her confidence makes them follow.

At evening roll call the girls are missed. Moodoo is immediately required to meet the Chief Protector. Before he does, though, we get a glimpse of the poor conditions of the workers' camp where he lives. It makes a clever visual comment on how those administering the protection policy neglected their duty of care towards those they were supposed to look after: while decisions about whether people could buy another pair of shoes, marry, or keep their children were made for them, they were kept in squalid conditions. Seeing Moodoo living this way makes his desire to be near his daughter even more poignant.

The girls run through the landscape in the storm, navigating it with some skill and, as Molly predicted, the rain covers their tracks. As the daylight fades, we come across the girls curled up on the riverbank, asleep, blended into their landscape. Molly sleeps soundly in a way she couldn't in the dormitory. The music is gentle to set the mood as one of peace. We get a strong sense that they are back where they belong.

Back in his office, Neville learns that the girls have been gone for two days. He worries that Molly has too much of the Aboriginal way in her, she is 'too much of their mind'. He is also worried about negative publicity: 'it must be kept out of the newspapers.' There is an undercurrent of menace in this scene for the stakes are high for Neville; there is the implication of a harsh response awaiting Molly's return, of the measures that might be needed to change her from being 'too much of their mind'.

## Walking home

Moodoo, meanwhile, is in pursuit of the girls. But Molly has natural instincts, bush smarts and skills. She diverts him first by using Daisy's bag to throw him off their track, making him think they have gone in a different direction, and then by walking in water, knowing that they can't be tracked that way. Molly's bush knowledge is to her advantage and we see that, even though she is a young girl and Moodoo an experienced tracker, she has a real chance of escape and avoiding capture and a fate like Olive's. But Moodoo works out Molly's plan and we see him smirk. Is this the self-satisfied look that comes with having worked out their tricks? Perhaps. But I prefer to read it as the first grudging sign of respect for a young girl who knows the tricks of the bush in a way that is a match for him. It is a testament to Gulpilil's skill as an actor that he can convey both simultaneously.

The girls meet some Aboriginal men who have been hunting. They know that the girls have escaped from Moore River and ask them where they are going. Jigalong, one says (David Ngoombujarra), is 'proper long way'. While they give the girls meat and matches, they don't give any further assistance. But they are strangely confident that the girls will be alright so long as they can outwit the tracker.

To remind us where the girls are, Neville's pen in close up traces lines on a map, showing us how far they have travelled and, from a discussion between Neville and the Police Inspector (Roy Billing), we discover that the girls have now been gone for over a week. We also learn that while Neville has the power and the duty to protect them, he has a limit to his resources. There is not a lot of money to pay for the search but the police agree to assist by spreading word of the escape. The news reaches Maude in Jigalong, and she seems unaffected. But when the camera catches her lost in her own thoughts, we see her almost smile. She knows Molly's strengths. And we know she has hope—almost a conviction—that she will see her daughters again.

Meanwhile, still a long way from Jigalong, Molly is caught stealing eggs from a barn by the farmer's wife (Edwina Bishop). She is stern with Molly, not at all friendly, but nevertheless gives the girls coats and food. She, her husband and their daughter, who we see studying on the porch, all seem unsurprised by the arrival out of the blue of three very young unaccompanied Aboriginal girls. The woman hurries them off, telling them to watch out for the men hunting rabbits along the fence. As Molly hears this, her face reveals a comprehension that this is the fence that connects to home.

I found this scene puzzling at first, just as I did when the Aboriginal hunters offer some assistance, but only go so far. The woman scolds Molly but also helps her and doesn't try to capture the girls or report them. The other thing that puzzled me is why give coats and food to the girls but do nothing more to help them on their journey? Does she, like the Chief Protector, see it's her role to protect them and make sure that they are safe? Thinking more about it, I see that her blonde daughter is the image of idealised childhood and has everything that Neville supposedly wants for all the Mollies, Gracies and Daisies he is supposed to protect but which the Moore River Native Settlement was incapable of providing. The scene offers an obvious contrast between the Aboriginal children who have been removed and the white child who does not have to worry about losing her family. It also shows that not all white people are bad: the farmer's wife is not a saviour, but she is more than indifferent. She helps, at least a little.

This scene is also undeniably a plot device—it is where the girls learn about the location of the rabbit-proof fence. The encounter has been a revelation for Molly. She explains to the other girls: 'find that rabbit fence, we go home'. The land and music sweep around them and we feel the determination, direction and confidence now that she has a clearer plan on how to find her way home. This is a very Hollywood moment. We now know that the girls have a clear plan for getting home. There was little sense before then, though, that they didn't know where they were going. They were always determined, always moving forward; at no time did we get the sense that they were lost. Now, however, Molly has an even clearer plan.

Back at Moore River, Nina reads a newspaper article aloud to the other children. Molly, Gracie and Daisy, we learn, have been travelling for about a month. The girls deride Mr Neville as 'Mr Devil' and cheer when they find out how long the girls have been able to evade capture. The fact that all that has been found of the girls is a dead rabbit is met with peals of laughter. The journey that Molly, Gracie and Daisy are on has begun to symbolise something important to the other children.

## Finding the fence

At this moment of public humiliation for Neville, the film cuts back to the moment the girls—and the audience—have been waiting for: Molly finds the fence! The girls run to it and hold it. Movingly, at this point there is a shot of their mother holding the fence miles further north at Jigalong. The fence is not just a pathway home, it represents an unbroken connection between mother and child, an umbilical cord. It is a symbol of reunion, of hope. But we don't get to savour hope for long.

By tracing the fence lines on a map Neville has worked out Molly's plan ('Just because these people have Neolithic tools … it does not mean they have Neolithic minds'). This means he now knows where they are. He sends a police officer from one direction and Moodoo from the other to capture the girls somewhere in the middle. As the film cuts between the images of the girls travelling the fence line and the men closing in on them, we fear that capture is imminent. Daisy's legs, scratched by the scrub, are hurting: how much longer can these girls keep walking this impossibly harsh land? But when Molly picks her up and carries her, we see how much strength she still has.

The girls also have a bit of luck. They meet a white fence worker (Ken Radley) who tells them of another fence (in fact, there are three in total) that will take them more directly to where they want to go and save them almost a hundred miles or so. In taking his advice, the girls inadvertently outwit Neville. This scene has that same puzzle for me as the one earlier with the farmer's wife and several others in which the girls meet adults. They all help the girls—but only to the extent that it does not inconvenience them. Not one does anything to return the girls to either the authorities or to their home. What is

Everlyn Sampi as Molly and Tianna Sansbury as Daisy.

the film telling us? Is it a sign of benign neglect on the part of white Australians? Does it reflect the ambivalence of an 'at least we are doing something' attitude, even if that something is ineffective? Or is the film showing us that although some white Australians in the 1930s might have wanted to help the Aboriginal families being torn apart, they too felt powerless in the face of the Act and the power of the authorities?

As the girls keep walking, they come to another isolated homestead. Here they meet Mavis (Deborah Mailman), a young Aboriginal domestic servant who recognises them from Moore River where she herself has been. She tells them they can sleep in her room and she will bring them some food. The full horror of Mavis's position is revealed when, in the middle of the night, the white farmer (Don Barker) tries to get into her bed. The presence of the girls frightens him off but we are left with the very clear understanding that sexual abuse is a normal part of Mavis's life. As she pleads with Molly—'Don't go Molly. He come back if you go'—the desperateness of her situation is clear. She is pleading with another child to save her and we know, that out here, she will never be heard, let alone saved. If the educated blonde daughter sitting on the porch of the earlier farmhouse scene offers the image of childhood that the policy was aiming to emulate, Mavis and her circumstance is the reality the girls could expect. Mavis is isolated and alone, without the support of family and cultural ties and also without opportunity or protection. This scene

Deborah Mailman as Mavis.

invites us to ask: is this the life that the authorities thought was better than life at a place like Jigalong?

While the girls are still with Mavis the police suddenly arrive and they have to flee. The authorities are closing in on the girls (but they will do nothing to help Mavis). At this point in the search, Moodoo appears to be aware of their hiding place but he does not give them away. Molly has used a number of ways to mask their tracks but we get the feeling that nothing can fool Moodoo. Has he decided that the girls have earned their freedom? Does he have respect for Molly's ability to outsmart the authorities? Has he always been ambivalent about his complicity in the role of capturing children and keeping them from home? Or has he had a change of heart and, now that she is so close to home, has come this far, is he reluctant to return her? Whatever his motivation, he changes from pursuer to rescuer and gives the girls the time they need to escape. His allegiance has swapped from the authorities to the girls.

## Whose problem?

Cutting back to Neville, we get a glimpse of his frustration as he speaks with the Police Inspector about the fact that the trackers have lost their quarry yet again. We also learn he has more vested in finding them than simply the return of three young Aboriginal children to the supposed security of Moore River: 'I will not have my plans put in jeopardy. People fail to understand that the problem of half-castes is not going to go away. [...] These children are that problem.' Molly, Gracie and Daisy are not just challenging Neville's personal authority, they have come to represent a challenge to all he stands for and believes is right: 'The cost is to more than just our pride', he says. 'The reputation of this department is beginning to suffer.'

Neville is portrayed with some sympathy in this scene. Flailing before Molly's determination to get home—the steely will of a child—he is forced to confront the evidence of the cruelty of the practice of separating children from their homes and families. If he allows her to succeed, if these three children demonstrate that the bond between parent and child is so strong that it cannot be broken, it means there is an argument to keep half-castes with their parents. And this, in turn, means everything he believes in is undone. It is his life's work, the work of a career. He has to stop them from getting back home: he sets a bait by telling the Inspector to send word out to the area that Gracie's mother is no longer at Jigalong but closer to where the children are at the small town of Wiluna, under 600 kilometres to the south of Jigalong.

Once again, we see Riggs and Moodoo waiting, planning an ambush. The landscape is vast, hot and hostile. The endlessness of what they see captured in Doyle's hand-held camera with long, sweeping shots, is metaphor for the enormity of the task white

Jason Clarke as Riggs.

Australians set themselves of taming this land and of removing the Aboriginal presence which is so entwined with the land, the enormity of the assimilation project. We get the first real confirmation of what we have suspected is Moodoo's growing admiration for Molly as he acknowledges how clever she is and marvels at her tenacity in getting back to her home.

## Losing Gracie
But just as the girls seem to form an unspoken alliance with Moodoo, they encounter an Aboriginal man (Heath Bergerson)

who, at the bidding of Neville, tells them that Gracie's mother is at Wiluna. While Molly's intuition warns her to be suspicious of this man, drawn by the overwhelming need to see her mother, Gracie heads to the nearby station to catch the train to Wiluna. The girls are separated for the first time since they started their journey. In Gracie's absence, Molly and Daisy start to struggle on their journey. It is not just their determination and their bush smarts that have kept them going this far; they have also been sustained by each other—their friendship, their shared goal, their shared fate.

The performance of Molly's despondency that Everlyn Sampi gives at this moment is extraordinarily powerful. It is very hard to remember that this is acting. Even harder to believe that this is her first-ever experience of acting on screen. Fretting for Gracie with what looks like a broken heart and a strong sense of her duty of care for her little cousin, Molly decides that she and Daisy can't leave her after all. But as they walk towards each other, a policeman and the Aboriginal man who had lied about Gracie's mother as he'd been told to, arrive in a car and snatch up Gracie, bundling her into the car. In a scene echoing the earlier one when the girls are first taken from Jigalong, Gracie is last seen through the back window of the car, looking back to the life—the family, friendships and bonds—that she is leaving behind. As Daisy pitifully says: 'She gone, Molly. She not coming back.' We don't see her again. This is the first time we see Molly cry. She knows that not only is Gracie lost to her but also that Gracie is now lost to her family. The exhaustion of the trip overwhelms her. She felt a responsibility for Gracie and feels that she has let her down.

The role the Aboriginal man plays in this turn of events is confronting. Why did he interfere in this way to thwart the girls' efforts to get home, especially when they are getting closer? What motivates an adult to play such a cruel trick on a child? Why cooperate with the authorities? Does he believe assimilation is the answer? How were his actions shaped by his own experience? Did he even have the power to refuse Neville's bidding? None of this is answered but these questions hang in the air as Gracie is lost to the Molly and Daisy.

Back on the fence, Riggs gives up his lookout and tells Moodoo that they should wait for the girls at Jigalong. Moodoo's expression is one of self-satisfaction. I suspect that Moodoo (and David Gulpilil) has enjoyed his switch in roles from being complicit with authority to subverting it. And more powerfully, he has seen, through the actions of the girls, how the very white authority that had kept him in his place could be challenged. This is the very message Neville was so afraid that the girls would send. In Moodoo's triumphant face, we see the girls have already bested not only Riggs, but Neville himself.

But Molly is unaware of these triumphs over authority. The loss of Gracie continues to take its emotional toll and the walk home from now on is relentlessly arduous and strained as the two girls drag their feet. And soon Daisy simply can't go on, so Molly has to carry her through a menacing and hostile landscape. Filmed in very little light, the colours are ominously dark.

## Nearing home

In the shots of the girls travelling the final part of their journey home, the landscape is very much part of the drama. Doyle's images and Gabriel's music meld together to create the atmosphere in which the land is hostile. It cannot be taken for granted. Not everyone will survive here; in fact, most people without an understanding of how to navigate this country would perish. In this way, the film makes sense of the knowledge the girls learned from their own culture shown in the earlier scenes where the older women taught their children how to find food and water, how to sustain themselves. This equipped Molly with the tools for this journey across this harsh landscape. But now, after such a long journey, and with the loss of Gracie, the struggle is greater. This culminates as the girls collapse from exhaustion.

*Rabbit-Proof Fence* is a film where the landscape is one of the characters. Giving the outback its personality and character is a hallmark of many Australian films. Perhaps it is because the relationship to land is so fundamental to all Australians, black and white. Or maybe it is because the land is such a force in forging our identity as a nation that it has something to say, some role to play, in so very many of our stories.

But it is not just the landscape that Molly and Daisy need to defeat in this last stage of their journey. Neville is still issuing his commands, ordering their recapture once they return to Jigalong. This is the heartbreaking reminder that the Molly and Daisy could travel all this way simply to be taken away from their home again. They are truly powerless.

But as the film cuts between the exhausted girls and their mother and grandmother waiting for them at Jigalong, the unyielding yearning for family gives a glimpse of hope. When Molly's spirit bird appears, then there is real hope: her grandmother has sung, sending the bird to help. Molly gets her final strength from the spirit bird and it guides her home. The women in Jigalong seem to know that the girls are close by and they chant to bring them safely home. Riggs notices the restlessness and activity in the camp and approaches the women, curious but almost fearful; their behaviour is unsettling him. He has worked among these people but he still does not understand them. Riggs thinks he sees Molly and Daisy in the bush but he is mistaken; it is only Maude and her mother. Armed, he asserts his authority and power but Maude is unafraid. She threatens him with a spear and he backs down.

Maude's behaviour does not surprise. Her daughters were taken from her by stealth and without her consent but she fought for them and she's not going to give up the fight now. Riggs's surrender, however, is unexpected. Is he exhausted by his attempts to capture the girls? Has he, like Moodoo, changed his views of the policy after seeing Molly's determination to return home? Are men in authority cowards when faced with the anger of the people whose lives they are regulating?

## Home

The spirit bird hovers closer over Jigalong and the women know the girls are near. Molly whistles its call to signal her return. As the slow motion and the sonorous music heighten emotions, I am overwhelmed by the reunion when it comes. The girls and their mother run to each other, silhouetted against the evening sky. As they reunite Molly's first words are about losing Gracie: 'I lost one' she sobs on her mother's breast. But the soft wailing is filled with joy as the girls are reunited with their family and they are home again.

Neville, of course, will not give up. He dictates another directive to Constable Riggs about his lack of funds to keep searching for the girls. Riggs has not told him they have arrived at Jigalong; Neville is in the dark in more ways than one.

He laments that 'we face an uphill battle in protecting the natives against themselves. If they would only understand what we are trying to do for them.' This final word from the authority of Neville foreshadows the justification of the policy after the stories of the cruelty and injustice became public knowledge: 'It was for their own good'; or 'It was done with the best of intentions.' There is an interesting reveal here about the official attitude towards the assimilation policy. Neville genuinely believed in the rightness of what he was doing. The reference to the lack of funds to support it showed the tension that occurred across the country between the large scope of the regulation of the lives of Aboriginal people and the lack of funds allocated to implement it.

## Last words

The film ends as it begins, with the real Molly Craig speaking in her language, a symbol of the closure of her journey back home and her reconnection to her culture. What happened in the rest of Molly's life is no less astonishing than the story we have just seen. After the nine week walk to Jigalong, she hid in the desert, married, had two girls, Doris and Annabelle, and then once again found herself back at Moore River Native Settlement. And once more she left, walking all the way back to Jigalong. Gracie, we learn, died: she never did make it home to Jigalong. But Molly and Daisy still live at Jigalong.

Once again there are no English subtitles. The aerial shots of the land, and of the real Molly Craig and Daisy Craig Kadibil, now two very elderly women, walking on their land, looking strong and defiant, tell us all we need to know.

The film ends in a similar way to how the film starts, with captions. The first one is about Neville:

The rabbit proof fence

Return journey

> Mr Neville was Chief Protector of Aborigines
> in Western Australia for 25 years. He retired in 1940.

The very last words are about the people who the policy he believed in damaged but ultimately failed to destroy:

> Aboriginal children were forcibly removed from their families
> throughout Australia until 1970.

> Today many of these Aboriginal people continue to suffer from this destruction of identity, family life and culture. We call them the Stolen Generations.

The word 'we' in this last sentence is a final powerful statement by Noyce, a unifying term that reveals a particular political perspective. And his use of the plural for 'generations' asks us to think about just how many stories there are like Molly's, Gracie's, Daisy's, Maude's, Nina's and Mavis's in that legacy.

The first credit, fittingly, is to Doris Pilkington Garimara. It simply says:

> Based on the book
> by
> Molly's Daughter

I like that Noyce gives her this honour. It is a testament to her tenacity to tell this story.

# VI

## DIFFERENT AUDIENCES
## DIFFERENT RESPONSES

There was a time when the removal of Aboriginal children was not a well-known part of Australian history. As I mentioned earlier, when I was at school, my classmates had never heard of the practice—they didn't know the policy had existed, that it was so prevalent, or its legacy so damaging to so many people. But ignorance is no longer possible.

I'm not claiming this is entirely due to the film. At least some of the credit for this should go to the 1995 *Bringing them home* report. The most powerful thing about this report is that it published many personal accounts of Aboriginal people who told what it was like for them as children who were taken away and as parents who lost their children. These moving accounts tell of the prolonged mourning that parents went through and of the extraordinary lengths they went to, trying to recover their children from state care. They tell of the children who suffered psychological, mental, physical and sexual abuse within institutions, in the families they were fostered or adopted out to, or in the workplaces they were sent to. The accounts are harrowing. Who can read them and not be affected? What they show is that you can make all the pretty legal and ideological arguments you like about why a policy is wrong and cruel but nothing is more persuasive than reading the legacy it has left on the people subjected to it by reading their own words.

## Caught in the crossfire

The official response to the report from John Howard's Liberal-National Government was to say dismissively that it was only one in ten children who were taken away, that many were removed for their own good, or at least removed with the best of intentions, and that the report was too emotive, using the term 'cultural genocide' when it was clearly not appropriate. It seemed to me at the time—and still does—that this sort of response was largely designed to detract from the personal narratives within it. Saying 'it was only one in ten' is a way of using statistics to undermine the power of the personal experience.

Of course, not every child had a bad experience. Many grew up in loving homes. And some were rescued from circumstances where they were being neglected. But that was not the totality of experience and it should be a concern that any child was abused or mistreated whilst under the care and protection of the state: it is callous to be dismissive of that. So much of what we see happening to Molly, Daisy and Gracie—and the film's Nina and Mavis—happened to those who spoke up for the *Bringing them home* report. And for many children it was even worse. The personal stories include accounts of continual sexual abuse, physical punishment and humiliating treatment akin to torture and psychological abuse. These things should never have happened.

I've long felt that the debate about how Australian history deals with this policy of removing Aboriginal children from their families has been and still is so hotly contested because it goes to the heart of the story that Australians tell about their history which tells us who we are and what our nation stands for. The struggle in the 'culture wars' or 'history wars', as it became called, was between two competing narratives about how we tell Australian history—do we romanticise our past or do we acknowledge the mistakes we have made? Are we black armbanded or white blindfolded? In truth it is never that simple: the debate about our nation's history is much more shades of grey than black and white. But the ideological warriors in the culture or history wars didn't seem to want to take any prisoners.

*Rabbit-Proof Fence*, being a film and so one of the most powerful ways of telling a story about the removal policy, was always going to be caught in the crossfire of those debates. And caught it was.

## The critical response

The world premiere for *Rabbit-Proof Fence* took place in February 2002 in front of almost a thousand people at Jigalong. It is the first film that Molly and Daisy had seen on a cinema screen. It must have been some night, under the stars. From this most humble of beginnings, the film would go on to be both a critical and commercial success. Noyce showed that it was no longer possible to say that Australian audiences would not go and see films about black people.[16]

Most critics responded to the deftness of the storytelling on subject matter that could have easily been preachy and heavy handed. US critic Sean O'Connell thought 'Noyce makes the right decision not to bog *Fence* down in political squabbles and race issues. [...] Instead, *Fence* gives us a cause we can all get behind: a marathon journey home.'[17] Others, however, understood that this was a movie that had a powerful point to make. As David Stratton observed: 'Perhaps the film lacks a touch of poetry, a grandness. But it is an important, and beautifully made saga, which provides plenty of food for thought.'[18] The Triple J radio critic also saw the power of the film:

> It is powerful, artistic and compelling, and not a bad home-coming for Noyce [...] the film's distorted visual perspectives and nightmare soundscapes give the viewer an even greater insight into the land, the hearts and minds of both its indigenous and white settler characters. [...] A big film about one of Australia's biggest secrets.[19]

It was, perhaps, overseas viewers, those least familiar with the policy, who were most astounded by the story. Respected US reviewer Roger Ebert compared the emotional impact of the film to Steven Spielberg's movie *Schindler's List* that tells the true-life story of a man who saved his Jewish workers from the Nazis:

> The final scene of the film contains an appearance and a revelation of astonishing emotional power; not since the last shots of *Schindler's List* have I been so overcome with the realization that real people, in recent historical times, had to undergo such inhumanity.[20]

Stephen Holden writing in *The New York Times* agreed:

The spic-and-span wholesomeness of *Rabbit-Proof Fence* ultimately makes its sting all the sharper. Its portrait of people who see themselves as decent, self-righteously trying to eradicate another culture, has the impact of a swift, hard slap in the face.

Along with these critical achievements, this is the film that took the story of the stolen generations to the world.[21]

## White blindfolds, black armbands

But this film with its simple story about three girls finding their way home would soon find itself in the midst of a debate about Australian history, Aboriginal history, and the extent to which a film that dramatically represents history can take liberties in that storytelling. Its subject matter that looked into Aboriginal assimilation policy became the target for many of those who had been involved in the debates that had arisen around the *Bringing them home* report.

The film became a lightning rod for the broader debates that had raged about the number of children removed, whether it was done for their best interests and whether it was a form of genocide. *Rabbit-Proof Fence*, being such a powerful story that sympathised with the plight of stolen children, was a source of great irritation for those who had relentlessly denied that the stolen generations existed. These criticisms are best laid out in the internet resource created by historian Peter Cochrane, *Rabbit-Proof Fence: the Question of the 'Intent' in History*.[22]

I am not going to be overly distracted by those debates as they are well articulated elsewhere.[23] And in my personal engagement with the film, those debates did not infringe on the way the film affected me. I have my own family history that includes stories of removal and perhaps this was why the debates about whether the stolen generation occurred or not seemed academic and clinical, removed from the reality of the stories that I had been told by my own family members. Those family stories—and those of other members of the community—seemed a much realer account of the impact and implications of the stolen generations' experiences than debates amongst commentators and historians in academic journals and conservative newspapers.

At the end of the day, the debates between academics and public intellectuals might shift public debate about the stories that get told about Australian history, might shift the ground in the tussle between white blindfold and black armband. But it seems to me that Aboriginal history—as Aboriginal people see it—is unchanged by those debates. The national narrative that is told about Aboriginal history—whether we are 'settled', 'conquered' or 'invaded', whether it was a 'stolen' generation and whether it was 'generations'—may be the subject of intense debates but those are debates amongst non-Aboriginal people. And these debates about the national narrative, the story the nation tells about its history are not really about Aboriginal history. They are debates about non-Aboriginal history and—intricately entwined with that—the identity of non-Aboriginal people. How Aboriginal people see their history remains largely unchanged by those debates and shifts amongst non-Aboriginal Australians.

A large part of the attack on the film was about what was claimed to be a lack of factual accuracy: the girls were taken by boat in real life, not by train; the camps were much more squalid; the children didn't follow the exact same route; it ignores what Doris wrote about Molly being ostracised by the full-blood members of her tribe; and the three girls were not removed in the highly emotive way that the film depicts.[24]

Another criticism of the film was that it failed to appreciate that the policy of removing children from their families was executed with the best of intentions and often for the good of the children.[25] But I'm far from alone in seeing the portrayal of A.O. Neville a man who is doing what he sincerely believed was best for the Aboriginal people in his charge. The film makes it very clear, for example, that one of his concerns over Daisy was that at such a young age she had been promised in marriage to a 'full blood' man. For those who want to see, *Rabbit-Proof Fence* shows that the policy of removing children was considered by some to be a humane solution to the 'half-caste problem', and that this was a problem for all Australia, not just Aboriginal Australians.

But whether removal of individual Aboriginal children from their families was for their own good or not, some things cannot be disputed. From the 1900s, the Northern Territory and most Australian states had legislation which regulated the lives of Aboriginal people and which often used the word 'protection' as the justification for such regulation. It is a cruel irony that legislation about protecting Aboriginal children had as a central tenet a policy that removed Aboriginal children from their families. Thousands of children were taken from their families either forcibly or in circumstances where they were tricked. Many parents tried desperately to reclaim their children. The philosophical driver was a belief that it was most desirable to assimilate Aboriginal children into white society.

The policy specifically targeted half-caste children and most families only lost their light-skinned children—what conclusion can be drawn from this other than that the legislation was driven by the idea that the Aboriginal race could be bred out? Logically, if the policy was really about 'bad mothers' *all* children whose mothers were considered not good enough would have been taken—those with dark and light skins.

Some children were placed in families in which they were happy. Many others were in orphanages or children's homes or sent out to unkind or cruel families where they were psychologically, physically and sometimes sexually abused. The impact of what happened left a lasting legacy on those who were removed, their families and communities.

## History, memory, storytelling

No film, not even a documentary (which *Rabbit-Proof Fence* doesn't pretend to be), can do anything other than *represent* reality—it can't *be* reality. Films use metaphors and symbolism as a means of telling a story and of making sense to their audiences. They use close-ups for example, to show a small part of a person, a thing or a place, to indicate the whole. They also use images and sounds to call up an attribute of that person, thing or place. We all read a film differently and clearly some critics saw things that others didn't. Equally, some critics wanted the film to be something other than it was. But Noyce's film explores all the aspects of the removal policy I've just listed and it uses images, sounds and words in dramatic, often poetic, ways. It uses these ways—many of which are specific to film—to tell a story and evoke ideas and feelings to show and tell the story of Molly, Daisy and Gracie. It also uses them to show something of the larger story of what happened over about 70 years to hundreds upon hundreds of Aboriginal children, their families and communities from the

Tianna Sansbury as Daisy, Everlyn Sampi as Molly and Laura Monaghan as Gracie.

late nineteenth century to the late 1960s when State governments removed mixed-descent Aboriginal children from their families, often by force.

Building on a screenplay that builds on a book that itself builds on experience and memory, Noyce gives Molly's story filmic text and texture. While he rejected a literal interpretation of Doris's book, acknowledged both with the change of title and the use of the words 'based on' in the credits, the aspects of the story that have been fictionalised have been done with reference to other published accounts.

Of the criticisms levelled at the film, the most interesting is about the portrayal of A.O. Neville. He was a formidable figure and spoke often of his views that are on the public record. Neville openly believed that the policy of removing children from their families was in the best interest of the half-caste children:

> The chief hope [...] of doing our human duty by the outcast is to take the children young and bring them up in a way that will establish their self-respect, make them useful units in the community and fit to live in it according to its standards.[26]

Neville's son, John Neville, was angered by the depiction of his father. He was aware that his father believed in assimilation and in a policy that would move 'half-castes' into white society which would result in the eventual disappearance of the Aboriginal race, but he accused the film of neglecting to portray an accurate picture of his father who had had a lot of respect for full-blood Aboriginal people. He also argued that the film was historically inaccurate because it failed to show that many Aboriginal people had loved the Moore River Native Settlement, that it had given them opportunities for education and work.

Kenneth Branagh's portrayal certainly captures Neville's belief in the need to assimilate half-castes. It doesn't, however, show that he had respect for full-bloods, or for Aboriginal culture. Nor does the film take the view that Aboriginal people liked the Moore River Native Settlement (Molly certainly doesn't), or that it was a place that set them up well for life (we only have to look at Mavis's fate).

The differences between the real A.O. Neville and the filmic character can be explained in two ways. Firstly, we are not seeing A.O. Neville neutrally or from his own point of view: he is interpreted through the eyes of the young Molly and other Aboriginal characters. Secondly, the film treats him more as a symbol than an embodiment of the real person and when developing the script, decisions were made to enhance the drama by playing with his character. Branagh added more nuance by giving a psychological interpretation of the character he was playing that hinted Neville had more at stake in recapturing the girls than might at first be thought.

Storytelling gives the creator a great deal of creative licence. Using actual historic figures is always tricky ground. In *Rabbit-Proof Fence*, there was a lot imposed upon A.O. Neville. He carried the mantle for the policies that it was his job to implement. It is easy to see why a family member would be less forgiving about literary or cinematic licence taken than other audience members.

I am not sure that the best reading of *Rabbit-Proof Fence* is one that simply labels Neville as a racist. That's too easy and cheap a shot. Together, Noyce and Branagh portray him as a man motivated strongly by the belief that the policy was the right one. The inevitable tragic consequences of that policy he may well have thought were worth it in the long run.

But we are entitled to look back and say that some of the things that happened were wrong and shouldn't have happened. We should always be asking ourselves whether policies should be improved; we should be constantly critiquing and analysing to learn what works and what doesn't work in order to achieve better results. This is especially true for policies in areas that most directly affect people's lives. It is hard to think of a policy more intrusive into family life than the removal of children.

## Repeating mistakes

In fact, it is much easier to be critical of past policies when we look at them with a contemporary gaze. The more pressing question is, to what extent are we repeating the mistakes of the past today? When Prime Minister Kevin Rudd delivered his famous apology speech on 13 February 2008, he said:

> The truth is: a business as usual approach towards Indigenous Australians is not working. Most old approaches are not working. We need a new beginning—a new beginning which

Kenneth Branagh as A.O. Neville and Roy Billing as the Police Inspector.

contains real measures of policy success or policy failure; a new beginning, a new partnership, on closing the gap with sufficient flexibility not to insist on a one-size-fits-all approach for each of the hundreds of remote and regional Indigenous communities across the country but instead allowing flexible, tailored, local approaches to achieve commonly-agreed national objectives that lie at the core of our proposed new partnership; a new beginning that draws intelligently on the experiences of new policy settings across the nation.[27]

And so we should learn from the lessons of the past and not keep policies that don't work. We need to move away from the old approaches. At the same time as Rudd spoke these words, however, his government was continuing to roll out a policy of top-down Intervention in the Northern Territory that suspended the *Racial Discrimination Act*, imposed compulsory income management and deprived Aboriginals of some basic human rights that other Australians continued to enjoy. Despite evidence from a range of sources, including the Government's, that this policy has not delivered results, the Federal Labor government has continued along this policy path. Today, in the Northern Territory (NT), the following is happening:

- **Child removal**: there has been a 69% increase in children getting taken into out of home care since 2007. Most are cases of 'neglect'. The NT, moreover, has the lowest rate of placement with Aboriginal families in Australia.
- **Attempted suicide and self-harm**: Incidents are being reported at 5 times the rate of 2007. In 2007 there were 57 incidents, in 2010 there were 183, and in 2011 there were 261.

- **School attendance**: Rates are down in preschool, primary and secondary schools. Overall, attendance rates have dropped from 62.3% just before the Intervention to 57.5% in 2011.

- **Incarceration**: Since March 2011 there has been a 40% increase in Indigenous incarceration. Recent reports suggest this number is now greater than 50%—with particularly large increases since mid-2011. The Prison Officers Association in the NT reports that inmates—the vast majority of whom are Indigenous—are being held in third-world prison conditions. There are 12–14 in a cell in Alice Springs with mattresses on the floor and a single hand basin and toilet between inmates per cell. Aboriginal people are one of the most incarcerated on the planet. If the NT was a country, it would have the second highest rate of incarceration in the world after the USA.

- **Housing**: Before the Intervention the rate of overcrowding was 9.4 people per home. By mid-2012 it was 9.3 (a decrease, but hardly an impressive one after five years, especially given the high levels of overcrowding).

- **Domestic Violence**: Police report incidents in areas subjected to the Northern Territory Intervention have dramatically increased since the Intervention and continue to increase—from 939 in 2010 to 1109 in 2011.

- **Alcohol**: the number of police incidents involving alcohol has consistently increased since the Intervention was introduced. The number of domestic violence incidents involving alcohol has also consistently increased. The government has no hard evidence that less alcohol is being consumed in 'prescribed areas'.

When I watch *Rabbit-Proof Fence*, I don't find myself challenged by A.O. Neville. He is a symbol of a past policy. What the film and his characterisation prompt me to ask is this: how much better are we doing today? And as the statistics above show, the answer is grim.

## The need for imagination

It is not surprising that Noyce and Olsen felt obliged to defend *Rabbit-Proof Fence* against the criticisms. But they make their most convincing arguments on film. It is the final scene of the movie where we see the real Molly and Daisy walk across the screen that I find the most persuasive. It is a reminder that this film has at its heart a true story, that beyond the politics and the policies there were three girls who wanted to see their mothers so badly that they walked through the desert for nine weeks all the way home, outwitting the authorities. And whatever the speculation about whether they were wanted as children, what is clear is that they loved the land and the community that they were born into. Not only did they walk across the continent to get back there; they stayed there, lived there, for the rest of their lives.

Doris heard the story of the girls' journey from her mother. Like most family stories told around a table or a campfire, stories handed down as family history don't shift because of the debates raging within opinion pages of newspapers or behind the walls of academia. Within the families of the people who lived those experiences, the stories remain unchanged by ideological debates. There is something very powerful in this thought. It means that, as long as we keep telling those stories, they will survive the ideological swings of the broader community.

None of the attacks on *Rabbit-Proof Fence* have altered the visual power the film has over me nor has it changed how I feel about the incredible journey that Molly, Gracie and Daisy took. It doesn't stop me from admiring Molly and Maude, feeling desperate for

Mavis and Nina, adoring of Gracie and the pixie-like Daisy, and moved by the scene when mother and daughters are reunited. In fact, I am reminded of something a friend once said to me: 'a writer needs to have an imagination; and an audience has to have one, too.'[28]

# VII

## THE LAST STEP OF THE JOURNEY

As I've already mentioned, one of the most moving moments in *Rabbit-Proof Fence* for me is where the girls finally reach the fence, run towards it and hold it. We then see Maude holding the fence and we know there is an unbroken connection between mother and child. It is one of those moments that shows why film is such a powerful medium of storytelling and it sums up the heart of this story.

It is not a story about politics and policy. It is a story about the strength of family and the connections to community and country. This is a universal theme, one we can all relate to but *Rabbit-Proof Fence* tells it in what is really a very simple way—three girls are taken away from their families and decide to walk all the way home. And it is this universal theme that I think is the pull of the story. It is told as an Aboriginal story; the journey is facilitated by the policy of removing Aboriginal children from their families. But the love between parent and child and the role that family and a sense of home and place plays in our identity and sense of self is a human yearning that knows no cultural or racial bounds.

And perhaps that is why so many people felt this was a story that just had to be told. I think that is what inspired Doris

Pilkington about her mother's story. I think that is why it appealed to Christine Olsen and it appealed to Phillip Noyce. None of these three saw this story merely as a political tool. Doris certainly didn't set out to write a political novel. She set out to write a story about her family. For Olsen and Noyce, it feels as though the politics are incidental. And today, the story remains as powerful as ever, timeless. Each time I watch the film, all that washes over me is the story. It remains untouched by the controversy.

The story that stays with me is the one told by Doris. I wondered why that was. It was Molly's story; Olsen wrote the screenplay; Noyce brought it to life. But it was Doris who crafted the first re-telling. It was she who, through all the family tales—and each family has thousands—that she heard, all the events in her own eventful life, all the stories she heard from her mother and aunt, she pulled out this one, remarkable feat. It is the intuition and skill of a great storyteller to pull out a tale and know its essence. And that is what Doris did. From this, Olsen could craft a rich and absorbing screenplay that allowed Noyce and the rest of his crew and cast to visualise it.

The result is an important piece of filmmaking. Not because it is such a successful movie—though it is that. Not because it showed that Aboriginal stories could be the subject of commercial films—though it did that, too. And not because as an artistic piece of work it is a finely crafted and beautiful film—though that it most certainly is.

The collaborative nature of Noyce's filmmaking, his ability to let the Aboriginal voice lead, something he learned from *Backroads*, meant that he could create a film that is true to the Aboriginal voices of Doris and her mother. Olsen's sensitivity to the subject matter, her relationship with Doris and Molly and her unorthodox

Top: Myarn Lawford and Ningali Maud Lawford. Below: Molly Craig and Daisy Kadibil.

wooing of Noyce created the basis for the collaboration and worked to keep the integrity of the Aboriginal perspective.

Noyce's collaborative way of working has been described as 'democratic'. But in the way that the Aboriginal voice is central in a story crafted for the screen by non-Aboriginal people, it is something more. It is an act of true reconciliation. And I believe that because I think a truly reconciled Australia is one where all Australians see Aboriginal culture and history as central to the whole nation's culture and history.

Noyce and Olsen saw Doris's book and Molly's story that way and they tell it as a story which is important not just to Aboriginal people but to all Australians. And they do so without appropriating the voices of the Aboriginal people. Doris and Molly remain centre stage, just as they should.

# NOTES

1. The Aborigines Protection Board was established in 1883 but given legal powers in 1909 by the *Aborigines Protection Act*. The Act gave the Board control over the lives of Aboriginal people, including the power to remove children from families. It was renamed the Aborigines Welfare Board in 1940 and finally abolished in 1969.

2. *Bringing them home: Report of the National Inquiry into the Separation of Aboriginal and Torres Strait Islander Children from Their Families*, also known as the 'Stolen Children' report, can be read in full at http://www.hreoc.gov.au/social_justice/bth_report/index.html

3. At http://www.landmarktheatres.com/Stories/rabbit_frame.html

4. Foley's screen presence makes the movie for me. He is one of my real life heroes. My second novel was set partially at the tent embassy in 1972 and the research gave me a chance to revisit his role in that era. I came to first meet him in person through my father and was always inspired not only by his politics but also admired his laconic style and his quick wit. I have to admit, as a teenager I was also quite afraid of him. For me, Foley embodies that era of energised political change. And in *Backroads*, we are reminded that, as well as being at the forefront of transformative politics from the 1970s, Foley would become an actor. He has, in recent times, revisited mixing politics and performance in his one-man show, *Foley*, in which he recounts stories from the years in which he set up the tent embassy, helped establish the Aboriginal Medical Service and the Black Theatre in Redfern and headed the Aboriginal arts board. The show was performed at the Melbourne Festival in 2011 and at the Opera House for the Sydney Festival in 2012. The radical firebrand has, over the years, become an iconic piece of living history.

5. Ingo Petzke. *Phillip Noyce: Backroads to Hollywood*. Sydney: Pan Macmillan, 2004, p. 61.

6. See http://www.kooriweb.org/foley/backroads/bkindex.html for more by Gary Foley on *Backroads*.

7. In 1976, a year before making *Backroads*, Noyce made two short documentaries which offer further evidence of his long-standing interest in Aboriginal issues. *Amy* is about a fifteen-year-old Aboriginal girl living in an inner city. It was part of film series, *Why Can't They Be Like*

*We Were?*, on themes around adolescence which were used as teaching aids in Australian secondary schools. In *God Only Knows Why, But It Works* Noyce filmed an outback doctor who used large doses of vitamin C to cure a range of illnesses. The film explores the neglect of Aboriginal health and the impact of misguided paternalism on the people who were supposedly being helped. It is a theme he would return to decades later in *Rabbit-Proof Fence*.

8. Petzke, p. 70.

9. Petzke, p. 326.

10. http://www.landmarktheatres. com/Stories/rabbit_frame.html

11. *The Sum of All Fears* was eventually made. Released in 2002, it was directed by Phil Alden Robinson and starring Ben Affleck and Morgan Freeman.

12. *Rabbit-proof Fence* Press kit, p. 12.

13. *Rabbit-proof Fence* Press kit, p. 14.

14. Petzke, p. 331

15. Indirectly, Gabriel had 'worked' with Noyce before. Over the end credits of his thriller *The Bone Collector* (1986), Noyce used Peter Gabriel's chart-topping song 'Don't Give Up' which he sang in a duet with Kate Bush. Memorably, Gabriel sang this song with Tracey Chapman at the 1990 concert to honour Nelson Mandela and a free South Africa.

16. In 2002, the Australian film *Crackerjack* made more money than *Rabbit-Proof Fence* and it is important to note that the total box office that year was the lowest it had been for 3 years. In all, only 4% of the Australian population has seen *Rabbit-Proof Fence* but it remains on school curriculums. It became one of only four Australian films about Aboriginal Australia to have made the all-time top 100: *Bran Nue Dae*, *Rabbit-Proof Fence*, *Ten Canoes* and *Samson & Delilah*.

17. Sean O'Connell, in filmcritic. com, review available online at http://www.eniar.org/news/ rpf-usreviews.html#fcc

18. David Stratton, 'The Movie Show', review available online at http://www.sbs.com.au/films/ movie/1073/rabbit-proof-fence

19. ABC's Triple J radio, transcript available online at http://www. abc.net.au/triplej/review/film/ s485339.htm

20. Roger Ebert, http://rogerebert. suntimes.com/apps/pbcs. dll/article?AID=/20021225/ REVIEWS/212250302/1023

21. Stephen Holden, 'Aborigine girls run away from a racist program', *New York Times* 29 November 2002.

22. See Cochrane's scrupulously balanced guide to these debates at http://www.hyperhistory.org/ images/assets/pdf/rabpdf.pdf

23. See Robert Manne, 'The Stolen Generations and the Right', *The Quarterly Essay.* Melbourne: Black Inc, 2001; Robert Manne, ed., *Whitewash. On Keith Windschuttle's Fabrication of Aboriginal History,* Black Inc. Books, Melbourne, 2003; Birch, Tony. '"This is a True Story": Rabbit-Proof Fence, "Mr Devil", and the Desire to Forget' in *Cultural Studies Review* 8.1 2002, 117–129; Hughes-D'Aeth, Tony. (2002). 'Which Rabbit-Proof Fence? Empathy, Assimilation, Hollywood', *Australian Humanities Review,* 14 June 2003; Emily Potter and Kay Schaffer, 'Rabbit-Proof Fence, Relational Ecologies and the Commodification of Indigenous Experience', *Australian Humanities Review.* Issue 31–32, April 2004; http://www.australianhumanitiesreview.org/archive/Issue-April-2004/schaffer.html

24. Peter Howson and Deb Moore, 'A Rabbit-Proof Fence full of holes' in *The Australian,* 11 March 2002.

25. ibid.

26. For more of Neville's writings see http://www.hyperhistory.org/images/assets/pdf/rabpdf.pdf

27. For the full text see: http://www.dfat.gov.au/indigenous/apology-to-stolen-generations/national_apology.html

28. Sue Abbey, the editor of my novel, *Home.*

# BIBLIOGRAPHY

Larissa Behrendt. *Home.* St. Lucia: UQP, 2003.

Larissa Behrendt. *Legacy.* St. Lucia: UQP, 2009.

Tony Birch. '"This is a True Story": Rabbit-Proof Fence, "Mr Devil", and the Desire to Forget.' in *Cultural Studies Review* 8.1 2002, 117–129.

Peter Cochrane, 'Rabbit-Proof Fence: the Question of the 'Intent' in History'. www.hyperhistory.org/images/assets/pdf/rabpdf.pdf

Roger Ebert, 'Rabbit-Proof Fence'. http://rogerebert.suntimes.com/apps/pbcs.dll/article?AID=/20021225/REVIEWS/212250302/1023

Stephen Holden, 'Film Review: Aborigine girls run away from a racist program', in *The New York Times,* 29 November 2002. http://www.nytimes.com/2002/11/29/movies/29FENC.html.

Tony Hughes-D'Aeth. (2002). 'Which Rabbit-Proof Fence? Empathy, Assimilation, Hollywood', *Australian Humanities Review,* Sept. (14 June 2003).

Peter Howson and Des Moore, 'A Rabbit-Proof Fence full of holes', in *The Australian,* 11 March 2002.

Human Rights and Equal Opportunity Commission. *Bringing them home: Report of the National Inquiry into the Separation of Aboriginal and Torres Strait Islander Children from Their Families.* Canberra: AGPS, 1997. www.hreoc.gov.au/ social_justice/bth_report/index.html

Robert Manne, 'The Stolen Generations and the Right', *The Quarterly Essay.* Melbourne: Black Inc, 2001.

Robert Manne, ed., *Whitewash. On Keith Windschuttle's Fabrication of Aboriginal History,* Black Inc. Books, Melbourne, 2003.

Sean O'Conell, 'Rabbit-Proof Fence', Rabbit-Proof Fence US reviews: http://www.eniar.org/news/rpf-usreviews.html

Ingo Petzke. *Phillip Noyce: Backroads to Hollywood.* Sydney: Pan Macmillan, 2004.

Doris Pilkington. *Caprice: A Stockman's Daughter.* St. Lucia: UQP, 1991.

Doris Pilkington. *Follow the Rabbit-Proof Fence.* St. Lucia: UQP, 1996.

Doris Pilkington. *Under the Wintamarra Tree.* St. Lucia: UQP, 2002.

Emily Potter and Kay Schaffer, 'Rabbit-Proof Fence, Relational Ecologies and the Commodification of Indigenous Experience', *Australian Humanities Review.* Issue 31–32, April 2004; http://www.australianhumanitiesreview.org/archive/Issue-April-2004/schaffer.html.

David Stratton, 'Rabbit-Proof Fence: Film Review', http://www.sbs.com.au/films/movie/1073/rabbit-proof-fence

## Filmography

*Backroads* (Phillip Noyce, 1977)

*Boat that Rocked, The* (Richard Curtis, 2009)

*Bone Collector, The* (Phillip Noyce, 1999)

*Bran Nue Dae* (Rachel Perkins, 2009)

*Crackerjack* (Paul Moloney, 2002)

*Dead Calm* (Phillip Noyce, 1989)

*Following the Rabbit-Proof Fence* (Darlene Johnson, 2002)

*Harry Potter and the Chamber of Secrets* (Chris Columbus, 2002)

*Last Temptation of Christ, The* (Martin Scorsese, 1988)

*My Week with Marilyn* (Simon Curtis, 2002)

*Patriot Games* (Phillip Noyce, 1992)

*Quiet American, The* (Phillip Noyce, 2002)

*Salt* (Phillip Noyce, 2010)

*Samson and Delilah* (Warwick Thornton, 2009)

*Sum of All Fears* (Phil Alden Robinson, 2002)

*Ten Canoes* (Rolf de Heer, Peter Djigirr 2006)

# CREDITS

## Key Crew

**Director**
Phillip Noyce

**Book**
Doris Pilkington Garimara
(*Follow the Rabbit-Proof Fence*)

**Screenplay**
Christine Olsen

**Executive Producers**
David Elfick
Jeremy Thomas
Kathleen McLaughlin

**Producers**
Phillip Noyce
Christine Olsen
John Winter

**Music**
Peter Gabriel

**Cinematography**
Christopher Doyle

**Editors**
Veronika Jenet
John Scott

**Casting**
Christine King

**Production & Costume Design**
Roger Ford

**Art Direction**
Laurie Faen

**Sound Design**
Craig Carter

**Children's Acting Coach**
Rachel Maza

## Key Cast

**Molly Craig**
Everlyn Sampi

**Daisy Craig**
Tianna Kadibill Sansbury

**Gracie Fields**
Laura Monaghan

**Moodoo**
David Gulpilil

**Molly's Mother**
Ningali Maud Lawford

**Molly's Grandmother**
Myarn Lawford

**Mavis**
Deborah Mailman

**Constable Riggs**
Jason Clarke

**A.O. Neville**
Kenneth Branagh

**Nina, Dormitory Boss**
Natasha Wanganeen

**Mr. Neal**
Garry McDonald

**Police Inspector**
Roy Billing

**Miss Thomas**
Lorna Leslie

**Miss Jessop**
Celine O'Leary

**Matron**
Kate Roberts

**Moodoo's Daughter**
Tracy Monaghan

**Olive**
Tamara Flanagan

**Kangaroo Hunter**
David Ngoombujarra

**Fence Builder**
Anthony Hayes

**Jigalong Depot Manager**
Andrew S. Gilbert

**Farm Mother**
Edwina Bishop
**Fence Worker**
Ken Radley
**Herself**
Molly Craig
**Herself**
Daisy Craig Kadibill

# Australian Screen Classics

'The Australian Screen Classics series is surely a must for any Australian film buff's library'
*Phillip King, Royal Holloway, University of London*
**Available from all good bookshops or from**
**www.currency.com.au**

*The Adventures of Priscilla, Queen of the Desert* by Philip Brophy
ISBN 978 0 86819 821 7
In his provocative reading of Stephan Elliott's cult 1994 film, Philip Brophy invites us to think more deeply about what this film is saying about Australia, its history, its culture and its cinema.

*Alvin Purple* by Catharine Lumby
ISBN 978 0 86819 844 6
Australia's first R-rated feature film created a furore when it was released in 1973. Catharine Lumby revisits claims that the movie is an exercise in sexploitation and argues the films complexity.

*The Barry McKenzie Movies* by Tony Moore
ISBN 978 0 86819 748 7
An illuminating tribute to Bruce Beresford's subversive and hilarious *The Adventures of Barry McKenzie*, and its riotous sequel, by cultural historian and documentary-filmmaker, Tony Moore.

*The Boys* by Andrew Frost
ISBN 978 0 86819 862 0
Andrew Frost's monograph explores the achievements of this award-winning film, placing its thematic concerns into a broader context of social anxieties about violence, crime and morality.

*The Chant of Jimmie Blacksmith* by Henry Reynolds
ISBN 978 0 86819 824 8
Based on Thomas Keneally's award-winning novel, Fred Schepisi's 1978 film is a powerful and confronting story of a black man's revenge against an injust and intolerant society.

*The Devil's Playground* by Christos Tsiolkas
ISBN 978 0 86819 671 8
Christos Tsiolkas invites you into Fred Schepisi's haunting film about a thirteen-year-old boy struggling with life in a Catholic seminary.

*Jedda* by Jane Mills
ISBN 978 0 86819 920 7
Many layers lie beneath *Jedda*'s surface and Jane Mills unpeels these, exploring the mysteries embedded in its story, soundtrack and images, making the film a classic of the Australian screen.

*The Mad Max Movies* by Adrian Martin
ISBN 978 0 86819 670 1
Adrian Martin offers a new appreciation of these classics: '*No other Australian films have influenced world cinema and popular culture as widely and lastingly as George Miller's* Mad Max *movies*'.

*The Piano* by Gail Jones
ISBN 978 0 86819 799 9
Writer Gail Jones' thoughtful and perceptive critique of Jane Campion's award-winning film, *The Piano*, assesses the film's controversial visions, poetic power and capacity to alienate.

*Puberty Blues* by Nell Schofield
ISBN 978 0 86819 749 4
'Fish-faced moll', 'rooting machine', 'melting our tits off': with its raw dialogue, Bruce Beresford's *Puberty Blues* has become a cult classic. Nell Schofield takes a look at this much-loved film.

*Wake in Fright* by Tina Kaufman
ISBN 978 0 86819 864 4
Tina Kaufman's essay explores how *Wake in Fright* was received on its first release in 1971. She also discusses the film's discovery after being lost for over a decade and its second release in 2009.

*Walkabout* by Louis Nowra
ISBN 978 0 86819 700 5
Louis Nowra says *Walkabout* 'destroyed the cliché of the Dead Heart and made us Australians see it from a unique perspective'.

*Wolf Creek* by Sonya Hartnett
ISBN 978 0 86819 9122
Sonya Hartnett weaves the fictional tale of *Wolf Creek* together with accounts of true murders and examines how the film is 'not simply a horror film, but a film in which horror happens.'